Praise for *My Uncle the Magician*

"Alex Nottingham conjures a spellbinding mix of heartfelt storytelling and practical insight. Every page elevates the ordinary into the extraordinary and leaves the reader inspired to serve at a higher level."

— Joseph A. Michelli, PhD, *New York Times* Bestselling Author, *The New Gold Standard* and *The Starbucks Experience*

"*My Uncle the Magician* rekindles the childlike wonder within us all. Like the rising phoenix, the story reminds us that true transformation begins within—by grounding ourselves in presence, cherishing each step of the journey, and trusting the unfolding of the Process."

— Sandy Jahmi Burg, Coordinator,
the International Focusing Institute,
and Author, *Smartview Stories*

"*My Uncle the Magician* is a thought-provoking story that tells us of the power of kindness, presence, and connection. Alex Nottingham offers a beautiful invitation to live more meaningfully and serve others with love."

— Piero Falci, Author, *A Better Life in a Better World* series

"This great book illustrates the mindful journey of meeting life's uncertainties with courage, curiosity, and open awareness. Alex Nottingham shows us that true strength lies not in accepting every answer handed to us but in questioning, exploring, and embracing the mystery with a fearless heart. A wise and inspiring story for anyone walking the path of awakening."

— Peter Strong, PhD, Mindfulness Psychotherapist
and Author, *The Path of Mindfulness Meditation*

"*My Uncle the Magician* demonstrates that true vitality isn't just physical—it's discovered in the joy, imagination, and human connection we seek every day. Alex Nottingham's story uplifts and energizes, showing how a spirit of imagination can fuel a life of lasting health and fulfillment."

— Uche Odiatu, Speaker on Wellness and Health
and Coauthor, *The Miracle of Health*

My Uncle *the* Magician

My Uncle *the* Magician

JOURNEY *from* HEARTBREAK *and* FEAR *to* SELF-LOVE

Alex Nottingham

MATT HOLT

Matt Holt Books
An Imprint of BenBella Books, Inc.
Dallas, TX

Matt Holt is an imprint of BenBella Books, Inc.
BenBella Books, Inc.
8080 N. Central Expressway
Suite 1700
Dallas, TX 75206
benbellabooks.com
Send feedback to feedback@benbellabooks.com

Matt Holt and *BenBella* are federally registered trademarks.

Printed in the United States of America
10 9 8 7 6 5 4 3 2 1

Library of Congress Control Number: 2026002027
ISBN 9781637749746 (hardcover)
ISBN 9781637749753 (electronic)

Editing by Lydia Choi
Copyediting by Scott Calamar
Proofreading by Denise Pangia and Becky Maines
Text design and composition by Jordan Koluch
Cover design by Ty Nowicki
Cover image © Adobe Stock / Maria Averburg
Printed by Lake Book Manufacturing

This book is dedicated to Mark, My Uncle the Magician.

Contents

The world is an illusion, it works by magic, and the magic is perception. And if you change the way you perceive, you change the way the world works around you. In other words, you change reality.

Author's Note

As you begin this journey, I'd like to share a simple invitation. *My Uncle the Magician* can be read in two ways:

- **As a story**—a novel you move through from beginning to end, allowing you to experience the story as you feel like a part of the journey.
- **As a practice**—a guide where you pause after each chapter to reflect, journal, or apply the lessons to your own life.

There's no right or wrong way to approach this book. Some readers will be content to enjoy it as a story. Others may choose to slow down, engage with the principles, and use it as a companion for self-discovery.

To help you along the way, I've created a set of free resources—including step-by-step tools, guided meditations, and additional materials—that you can access anytime at: https://alexnottingham.com/tools/.

And when you reach the end of the book, you'll find a summary of the core principles and more resources.

Wherever you are right now, start there. Read in the way that serves you best. My hope is that these pages spark insight, presence, and perhaps even a little magic in your own life.

—Alex Nottingham

My Uncle the Magician is the true account, as best my memory serves, of events and conversations that took place in real time between myself and my uncle Mark. However, some of what I recount has been embellished to create greater clarity as well as reader appeal and involvement. Descriptions of my inner visions, specifically, are written as I best remember them, and in some cases, names are changed to afford individuals' privacy.

PART 1

* * *

Tools and Teachings

CHAPTER 1

* * *

Meeting the Magician

Words are, in my not so humble opinion, our most inexhaustible source of magic.

—Albus Dumbledore,
Harry Potter and the Deathly Hallows: Part 2

When I first met my uncle Mark, I didn't know I was meeting the man who would become my greatest mentor. The man who would teach me that magic is real. That magic is universal, accessible by anyone and everyone. That it's both practical and mystical. But most importantly, what Mark taught me is that magic is hard earned. It isn't like a genie bursting forth from a bottle and granting you three wishes because you dusted off an old lamp. When it comes to my uncle's magic, what you put into it—faith, good intentions, and hard work—is what you get out of it.

I first met my uncle Mark when I was ten years old. A couple of years after my parents were divorced, Mark introduced my father to Elisabeth, the woman who would later become my stepmother. Mark's wife, Nice, is Elisabeth's sister.

I had little contact with Mark until one day when we were hanging out with my family in the living room at my father's house. When I actually spoke with Mark, I was immediately drawn to him, though I wasn't sure why at the time. Some of my family thought he was weird and that he had an eccentric personality, but he fascinated me.

Here was someone who seemed like a normal guy, a physician who watched college football and crime dramas, who had a slight Brooklyn accent and used Yiddish words befitting his Jewish heritage, who went snow skiing and played poker when he wasn't lounging around at home. Yet he talked to me about metaphysics, quantum mechanics, and philosophy. He made his own herbal remedies and supplements. He followed a mysterious system he called *the Process*, which he claimed had helped everyone from burnt-out executives to world leaders take their lives back and use their newfound energy to improve the lives of those around them.

I sat down next to him on the couch, squeezing between him and my father. I was brimming with questions. "So what happens to all of the matter that gets sucked into black holes?" I asked.

"There are different theories," Mark said.

"Like what?"

"Some say that the absorbed matter is infinitely compacted upon itself. Another theory suggests that the matter goes into another dimension or area of space-time. But we can—"

"What happens with white matter?" I interrupted.

"Alex, you're going off on a tangent."

"What do you mean by 'tangent'?" I asked.

"Look it up."

"You can just tell me," I said with a chuckle in my voice.

"That defeats the purpose," Mark insisted, his eyebrows arched. "Besides, it's important that you define what it is you're talking about. This provides the proper context."

I got up and went to my father's library, where I found an old *Webster's* dictionary. I proceeded to look up the word "tangent" as I walked back into the living room. I told Mark that a tangent was a geometric concept where two lines touch but don't intersect.

"Wrong!" Mark said. "Did you read the whole definition?"

"No," I said sheepishly.

"That's interesting. I can tell that you jump to conclusions."

"Why do you say that?"

"Because the world is a hologram, Alex. When you cut a hologram in half, each half contains the entire holographic image. In this and in life, the small reflects the whole." Mark continued: "When I asked you to look up the word, you gave me the first definition without reading further. This suggests you don't thoroughly examine issues before you act. Now find the definition in the context of our discussion."

I flipped through the pages again and read the last definition for "tangent": "To suddenly abandon one course of action or thought and shift to another."

"Exactly!" He clapped his hands together and smiled. Then he looked at me seriously. "Alex, you and I are very alike. We both have unstructured minds. We can be all over the place, less focused. But we can also be highly creative, hyperfocused, and full of potential. Either you will do something great for humanity or end up with a life full of drama. Thankfully you have some say in the matter."

I laughed, surprised by the way he talked to me. I didn't know anyone else who was so direct. I found it refreshing.

"Mark, play us something!" my father called out.

"Play 'Earth Angel'!" Elisabeth requested.

Mark walked into the piano room in my parents' house, a small, oddly shaped room filled with books and statues. He sat down at my father's baby grand piano in the center of the room and started playing, his hands gliding across the keys. He played "Earth Angel," "House of the Rising Sun," and numerous other songs with ease. I wanted to be able to do that too.

When he finished up the last song, "Love Potion No. 9," we all applauded and whooped.

I sat beside him on the piano bench. "Mark, I love the way you play! I tried to learn when I was little, but then I got so bored and just quit. You must have been playing your whole life."

"In fact, no." Mark pulled the polished black keyboard cover over the keys. "I just learned a system. You see, for my brain to work, I have to take complex things and make them simple. This also helps me teach others."

"I want to play like you," I said.

"You can. In fact, I could teach you how to play like me in just three lessons."

"Really?"

"Yes. Next weekend, come on by and I'll show you."

"I'll be there."

* * *

I went to Mark's house on a Saturday, and his wife, Nice, answered the door. "Hey, Alex! So glad you could come." She gave me a big, warm hug. "We have lots of food in the kitchen. Help yourself to anything you like."

After stuffing my face with pasta covered in a delicious pesto sauce, I reminded Mark that he'd promised to teach me how to play.

"Ah, yes," he said. "Let's begin the training."

We took a seat at his upright piano, which was made of a tan, antique-looking wood with gold accents. The leather on the seat was a bit worn but comfortable, nonetheless.

"First, Alex, you must understand the system. You have your right hand, which is the treble." He positioned his right fingers on the keys. "And your left hand will play the chords."

Then he placed his left fingers. "They call this *fake music.* It's a shortcut for playing beautiful songs without excessive practice or lessons. Now, what I will have you do first is—"

"What are all these little figures?" I interrupted, pointing to the top of the piano. The one that stood out the most was an old man in a bright-blue silk robe sitting on a brown chest, a pointed purple hat on his gray head of hair. His beard was wild and long.

"Oh, ha! That's Merlin. A gift a patient gave me depicting me as a magician. You see, I love magic. The world works like magic."

"So you do tricks and things?"

"You can say that. Ever since I was a child, I've done magic tricks for friends. I even tried some hypnosis."

"Hypnotize me!"

He laughed, his eyes almost closing completely. "Actually, you're already hypnotized."

"What? How am I hypnotized?"

"By your conditioning. What the world has imposed upon you and what your parents have projected on you. Your unwavering belief and attachment to those structures is why you're hypnotized. But enough of that." He smiled warmly. "In short, I do magic every day!"

"Yeah? Like what?"

"As an ob-gyn, I deliver babies, and my deliveries usually occur in a somewhat predictable pattern. At first I would find these coincidences funny, but experience after experience supports a world that has an order to it, which I call *magic*. And once I began training in the Process, delivering babies wasn't the only thing that occurred like magic."

I was glued to every word he said, in awe. *Magic? For real?* "You mentioned the Process," I said. "What is that? I'm sure you could teach it to me!"

"Maybe one day. But let's start with the piano first." He laughed.

Sure enough, as Mark had promised, I learned the piano in just three lessons. And for my birthday that year, Mark got me a book of over a thousand songs. I loved being able to play, sing, and create. Yet I was still so curious about this magic stuff he talked about.

One day when he was visiting at my dad's house, I asked him, "Now, how about you teach me some magic?"

"You're ambitious. Why do you want to learn magic?"

"So I can get what I want."

"What do you want?"

"Money, fame, power . . . Duh!"

"You're a schmuck," he pronounced, using the Yiddish word for a foolish person.

"Magic is defined as using the nonmaterial to affect the material world," he went on. "It can be positive or negative. What you're talking about is dark magic, which is using the nonmaterial for personal gain only. I don't teach the dark stuff, only the light. For example, the power of positive thinking."

"Positive thinking? What else do you teach?" I asked.

He patted my head, but somehow it didn't feel patronizing. "Maybe someday you'll be ready for the next lessons," he said.

Mark didn't tell me anything more about the Process at that time. In fact, he refused to—until years later, when I became desperate enough to ask for his help.

CHAPTER 2

* * *

Breakdown

There is no breakthrough without a breakdown.

—Tony Robbins

Years after I met Mark, my college girlfriend, Rachel, was driving us back to our University of Central Florida campus in Orlando along I-95. Every light we passed along the interstate briefly lit up Rachel's face, her pointed nose, and locks of thick brown hair that fell along her cheeks.

I reached out and put my hand on her leg, but I noticed her shoulders tense up. So I pulled my hand away and drummed my fingers on the door.

"What'd you think of the wedding?" I offered, looking out the water-spotted window. We'd just left my aunt Eliete's wedding in Palm Beach.

She turned the radio down. Genesis's "Invisible Touch" faded to a whisper. "It was fun. Your family's pretty cool."

After a few beats, she smiled. "I liked the singing. Is there always that much singing in the ceremony?"

"Yeah, that's the cantor. She also sings at the synagogue."

"Well, it was beautiful," she said. "Reminded me of the opera. Or at least, the one opera I went to with my mom. It *almost* made me consider having a Jewish wedding."

"Really?"

"Almost."

I tried to focus on the raindrops racing down the window to keep myself centered. I was getting nauseous again, like I had been on and off for months. I could feel the familiar tension building between Rachel and me. She absentmindedly fingered the cross hanging from her neck as she was driving. The silver chain looked beautiful against her emerald-green dress.

"You'd consider converting, right?" she asked. "Like, if we were getting married."

My stomach turned. I looked at Rachel through the corner of my eye. The truth was, I would convert for her. I'd always pictured a wedding ceremony in my culture, complete with the chuppah—a canopy under which a Jewish couple stands during the ceremony—and breaking the glass, and dancing the hora. But she was more important to me than the particulars of the wedding or even my faith.

It scared me to think of what I'd do to keep her. Sometimes I felt like I'd jump headfirst into a bottomless pit if she told me to. But I'd already told her so many times what I would do for her. So many times that this question had now started to feel like a little game. And I wanted to play it differently this time.

"Do you eventually *want* to marry me?" I asked, watching her face brighten and dim as we passed under the median lights.

She creased her eyebrows like she was deciding where to eat dinner or which shirt to put on. "I have no clue. I don't know if I even want to get married. If I decide to, there's a lot I want to do first. Graduate at least." She chuckled uneasily.

"Right," I said. "That's not . . . eh, never mind."

She shrugged and turned up the radio again, then changed it to a pop station. Nelly Furtado's "I'm Like a Bird" played through the buzzy speakers.

I leaned my elbow on the door and massaged my forehead, willing the throbbing pain and dizziness to go away. It felt like my head was stuck in a tire rolling downhill. And it seemed to get worse when I was around Rachel. "I guess what I'm asking is if you want to be with me for a long time. *After* college."

She shot me a blank look. "Come on! That's the same question."

"I don't think it is."

"Well, I don't have an answer. I want to be with you *now*. Isn't that enough?"

I could feel bile rising up in my throat. "Three years in, and you're still as unsure as you were when we started college?"

"I guess I am. Is that a problem for you?"

"Yes, it is. If you don't know now, then when will you?"

She shrugged. "Maybe when you stop asking me for validation, then acting like a hurt puppy when I don't give it to you."

Her words felt like a flaming arrow through the center of my chest. My face was getting hot, and my hands felt like they were on fire. But at least it dulled the nausea.

"Why are you even with me?" I snapped at her. "I know *I* want this. I know you're my future. It kills me that you don't feel the same way— *Oh crap, look out!*"

A red car had just swerved in front of us. Rachel yanked the steering wheel to the right, and we started skidding. I leaned over the center console and pulled the wheel back to the left to try to correct it, but she jerked it again to the right. We lost control and were sent spinning directly toward the barrier wall. Rachel was screaming, both hands on the wheel.

They say your life flashes before your eyes in moments like this, but mine didn't. Instead, time slowed to an extremely slow crawl, like watching a video in slow motion. A surprising calm came over me. I didn't feel afraid. I didn't scream or freak out. I just felt certain that there was more for me to do, that I wasn't done yet. And I had the distinct sense that, if I survived this wreck, I'd be stepping out of the car onto an altogether different path.

We crashed diagonally into the wall, her side taking most of the impact. A blast of white dust exploded from the car, the airbag in front of me blew up like a balloon, and then it was over, aside from the car's sluggish creaking.

A little disoriented, I opened the door and went to help Rachel get out of the car. She was shaking and had a few bruises but was otherwise okay. Her gray Hyundai Elantra was totaled, though.

As we stood around with the cops, waiting for the tow truck and a ride home, Rachel held up a black umbrella for us. Raindrops drummed on the fabric, echoing in the silence between us. I put my suit jacket on Rachel's shoulders and tried to keep my arms around her, but she stiffened up again, so I put my hands in my pockets.

"At least we're dressed for the occasion," I joked.

She kept her gaze on the highway. No hint of a smile or anything.

"Rachel . . ."

"What?" Her voice was tired and flat.

"You don't want this, do you?"

She scoffed. "A totaled car and whiplash? No, I don't."

"You know what I mean."

"This isn't the time."

"Don't think, just tell me."

The spring semester of our junior year was almost over. I knew we wouldn't see each other much over the summer—she'd go back to Fort Myers to her family, and I'd be on the east coast of Florida, where I grew up. It was only a two-hour drive, but I had a feeling that was too much distance for us.

She turned to me. "Fine. I think we should take a break. Just to get some space and figure things out. We can talk again next semester."

Her words made my stomach twist. "Okay" was all I could say.

She laughed darkly. "Maybe this wreck was a sign."

"Maybe," I echoed. "All I know is that after this summer, I'll be a new guy. I'm going to be better for you. In every way. I promise."

"There you go again." She shook her head, then met my eyes. "Don't just do it for me, Alex. Do it for you too."

As if on cue, my father pulled up onto the shoulder of the crash site at that moment. When we climbed in the back of my father's car, we found Mark in the passenger seat. He smiled when he saw us, his dark eyebrows raised as if amazed by something.

* * *

When the spring semester ended, I headed back to my father and stepmother's house in southeast Florida. I planned on spending the summer there playing tennis, working for my uncle John's furniture rental company, and hitting the beach as often as possible. Instead, I spent the first two weeks holed up in my room, glued to my twin-sized bed. I couldn't stop memories of Rachel from flooding in. It hurt like hell not to be near her anymore, more than I expected it would. We'd had our issues and plenty of fights. But now, only the good things seemed to have stuck with me—our trips to Disney, time with each other's families, late-night visits.

Despite myself, I called her every so often. Whenever

I asked about us, she'd just say, "Let's wait and see. Maybe next semester will be different."

In so many ways, this part of Florida was paradise. So every time I thought about how I must've looked, lying awake at 4 AM in my childhood bed with bloodshot eyes that wouldn't close, I had to laugh. I mean, this was just some college relationship, right? Sure, we'd been together for three years, and sometimes I felt I loved her so much that I'd jump into traffic if she asked me to. But at the end of the day, it wasn't anything to lose my mind over. At least, that's what I tried to tell myself.

One night, when I finally fell asleep around 3 AM, I dreamed I was lying face down on cold ground.

I felt a hot breath at the back of my neck and looked up to see a pair of red eyes inches away from me.

"Pathetic," the creature snorted, hot puffs of rancid breath covering my face with each syllable. "Aren't you supposed to be the straight-A student? The promising young man?"

I tried to run away but quickly tripped. It wrapped its tail around me and lifted me into the air.

"You like to run, don't you?" The entity grinned, the entirety of its face folded up like an accordion. "Do you think anyone respects a man who runs? Who cries and moans like you do?"

I beat my fists against its crushing tail. "Let me go. Please let me go!"

The entity bellowed with laughter. It sounded shrill and chaotic, like a hundred metal pots clanging together. It dropped me onto the ground, but I couldn't will myself to run again. I was frozen, my body invaded by the sound of its laughter.

"Alex, Alex, Alex," it said, lying down on its side near me. "You really aren't good for anything, are you?"

Moments later, I shot up in bed. Nearly hyperventilating, I wiped the sweat from my hairline and clutched my head between my knees, terror surging through me. I'd never had a dream that was so visceral, so real—the heat, the rancid smell, the tail squeezing my sides. It took me forever to calm down enough to take deep breaths.

That thing, whatever it was, hated me. Absolutely hated me. Saw nothing of worth in me.

Did I agree with it? I had to confront the fact that maybe I did. At least, some part of me did.

But where was this coming from? I had my whole life in front of me. Why was I so out of control? How could I get the pain to stop?

"Okay," I said out loud, bringing my hands down to my sides. "Okay. I have to do something about this."

I tried to get back to sleep, but the sun rose quickly before I could.

* * *

The therapist's couch was a brownish-yellow color that immediately made me nauseous when I saw it. After he got me settled, rather than taking the plush chair to the right of the couch, Dr. Friedman sat behind a big wooden desk. There was a square glass trophy on it for some local award he'd won, and I watched his hands through the glass as he shuffled papers around.

"Okay, Alexander, what brings you in today?" he asked brightly.

I grimaced. "My girlfriend broke up with me. I'm not eating, not sleeping. I think about her constantly."

"Mmm . . ." Dr. Friedman leaned his head on his hand, the skin of his cheek covering half his left eye. "Tell me more about those thoughts."

"Well, I think of her smile. I think of all the awesome memories we've made together. She just seems ready to give up on it all. I can see how good our future would be, a house full of kids, a big house, both of us happy with good jobs. Maybe it sounds clichéd, but I know she wants that too. And she's so beautiful, and I've never loved anyone—"

He held up his hand. "Let me stop you right there. Can't you see, Alexander? That's the source of your misery, all this thinking, all this . . . *intellectualizing*. You have to accept that it's over. And the first step is to stop your obsessive thinking."

I thought about that for a minute. And perhaps he was internally laughing at me as I *thought* about his advice. He had a few diplomas hanging on the walls. The books behind him seemed clinical and dense—none of the spines were skinnier than my forearm. And of course he was wearing thin-rimmed glasses that gave him an air of quiet authority.

It all seemed contrived. I felt like I'd seen him, this office, in countless movies, and I couldn't shake the feeling that it wasn't real. Not really.

"You're right. If I stopped thinking, I'd be happier. But how do I stop thinking?"

"Great question. Whenever a thought of this woman comes into your mind, just will it away. It's about willpower, Alexander."

I wanted him to stop calling me that. Only my parents called me that.

"Please call me Alex," I said with a slight hint of annoyance.

He quirked an eyebrow, then regained composure. "Okay, *Alex*," he said slowly and calmly. "As I was saying, it's about willpower. You have to *want* to get better, and then you have to take steps that get you closer to being better. And in this case, the first step is to stop all this useless thinking. If she's really gone, then there's nothing more you can do."

"Nothing more?" I said. "But she said she wanted a break. I'm not even sure it's really over. How can there be nothing more to do?"

"Let me put it this way." He interlaced his fingers on the desk—and *that* I had definitely seen in the movies. "In life, we're given two choices: We either keep moving forward or we get pulled back. The past is important for us to reflect on, but it isn't a place for us to live."

"Right."

"So, stop living there! Stop thinking and cultivate good

habits instead. Start reading more, or maybe go ride your bike. Don't sit in a bad feeling—resolve to change it!"

"Well, I guess I haven't played tennis much lately," I said.

He smiled. "There you go, son. Now, let's make a plan."

* * *

By the end of the session, I'd committed to Dr. Friedman's strategy. I played tennis with some friends in town, rode my bike more, ate at the dinner table with my dad and stepmother instead of in my room. And it did help. I felt motivated, even hopeful—for about a week. Then the thoughts once again took over my mind like leaves piling up on the lawn. I'd rake them away and more would take their place.

After a month of sessions, I was even worse off than before. Thoughts of her never seemed to stop, and nothing I did could make them go away. I wondered if I could've done more for her. If I could've been more for her. If something was wrong with me and she could see it better than I could. Why didn't she want me? What was wrong with me?

Soon, my anguish turned to anger. One day in early July, while my three-year-old sister, Vanessa, was out with my stepmother, I stormed onto the back porch and kicked her beach ball into the back fence. It was a pointless move. The ball barely bounced back, infuriating me more. I threw her Barbies against the porch wall. I stepped on her Cabbage Patch Kid. I don't think Vanessa, an actual toddler, could have thrown such a tantrum.

At some point my father came outside. I stopped raging, my chest heaving, and glanced sideways at him. He was wearing a white button-up shirt with thin red stripes. I could see the concern in the shallow creases at the corner of his eyes. His hair was edged neatly along his face.

"Alex, this has to stop," he said.

His composure made me feel a hundred times smaller. "I don't know what to do. I feel out of control. Therapy was a waste."

"I have an idea. Do you remember Mark?"

When my father brought him up, I thought of the step uncle who'd taught me piano so many years ago. We hadn't kept in very close touch since then, but he did provide me some nice advice my freshman year of college regarding Rachel, and we'd had that chance encounter after the car accident.

My father continued. "You know, he's been a great help to your stepmother and me. I think he can help you too."

Dad had told this story many times. He and my stepmother, Elisabeth, had been trying to conceive for years. They'd tried in vitro fertilization, hormone shots, even a few herbal concoctions. Nothing worked.

Mark's an ob-gyn, so you wouldn't be too surprised to hear he helped them. But it was the way he helped that was magical. He brought my father and stepmother into a meditation using the Process to see where the blockage might be. It turned out that my father wasn't sure he wanted another baby and was looking to retire.

Mark told my father, "You can choose to retire and give yourself a message that life is ending, or choose to start a new family, and that you have a whole new life to look forward to."

Once my father had broken through that barrier of concern, and Elisabeth felt the shift happen in them both, Elisabeth became pregnant with my little sister in a matter of months. The same little sister whose things I was now destroying. I hung my head.

Dad continued, "You'll have to ask Mark directly for help. I can't influence you, meaning it can't be my doing."

"Okay. I'll talk to him."

He pressed his hand against my back. "You'll get through this. You'll be right back on track by the fall. I know you will."

He nodded quickly, then went back into the house, leaving me alone, surrounded by a tornado of toys. I put all the toys back where I'd found them on the porch and straightened the Cabbage Patch doll's dress. Then I went to the old landline phone hanging on the wall in the kitchen and dialed Mark.

"Hello-o?" he answered in a singsong voice.

"Hey, Mark, it's Alex."

"Alex! Great to hear from you. What can I do you for?" His voice had a clear, even tone.

"To tell you the truth, I've been struggling lately. Dad says you might be able to help."

"Then I'm glad you called," he said brightly. "How about you come by on Saturday? And we'll see what we can do."

* * *

When I woke up on Saturday, my chest was heavy with dread, but I wasn't about to back out of meeting with Mark. Even the slightest hope that I could be pulled out of this rut was enough to get me moving.

I put on a UCF T-shirt, a pair of jeans, and white tennis shoes, and left the house by 9 AM. Mark lived about twenty minutes north of my father's house. It was a sunny day, and with my windows down I could smell the salt in the air. As I drove parallel to the beach, images of Rachel's face bombarded me. I could see us lying on a multicolored towel, Rachel looking off into the distance as she laughed, her dark hair dotted with sand, drops of ocean water shining on her olive-toned skin, me leaning in to kiss her shoulder . . .

"Geez, dude," I said out loud. "Get it together!" I slapped myself in the face a few times to make my point.

When I pulled into Mark's driveway, the garage door was open, the space inside framed like some movie scene you wanted to jump right into. Mark was at his long wooden worktable, scooping and pinching and pouring powders and oils into a variety of bottles and jars, bobbing his gray head along to the classic rock station on his radio. He popped rose hips into one jar with a flourish, turned around and scooped a green powder to follow it, singing along to every word of the fifties rock song that was playing. His dark-brown eyebrows were perpetually raised, as if everything amused him. I remembered Mark telling me that if he hadn't become a doctor, he would've been an actor or singer, going all out on Broadway stages or playing lively piano jams in smoky, raucous bars. He would've been damn good at it too.

As I got out of the car and walked toward him, Mark looked up and tipped an invisible hat to me. "Good to see you, Alex."

"You too," I said.

"I was just finishing up with my supplements." He pointed to a cream-colored powder in a small jar. "That's my protein blend for the week." He pointed to the taller bottle with the rose hips in it. "And this one's for tea. The roses came from Nice's garden. The lavender too. But enough about that. Come on, let's go get comfortable."

He motioned to the dark-green leather couch facing the back wall of the garage. An old boxy TV sat in front of it, as well as a coffee table with an ashtray and a cigar box. We sat on opposite ends of the couch, and Mark settled back into the corner.

"So, Alex. How can I help you?"

Strangely, I didn't feel the need to hold anything back. I told him all about the breakup, that I wasn't eating, my anger. I also told him that the therapist had given me some advice, but it wasn't helping.

Mark laughed. "Like everything else in the world, there are helpful and unhelpful therapists. What did yours say?"

"He pretty much told me to stop thinking. To just will the bad thoughts out of me."

Mark shook his head. "Suppressing your thoughts and

feelings just makes them stronger. Imagine taking an upset dog and throwing it in a room and locking the door. When you come back later, do you think the dog will be calm?"

"No, it'll be even more stressed," I said.

"Yes," Mark said. "Dogs go crazy in locked rooms, just like you would."

I knew he was making a good point, but why was he comparing me to an out-of-control animal? It seemed harsh.

Mark cleared his throat before continuing. "So, Alex, is it you or your father who wants me to help you?"

"Me. My father just suggested it."

"Okay, that's very important. You must never help someone who doesn't want to be helped. If you tried, you'd be stripping that person of their free will."

"How so?" I asked.

"You can offer to help an old lady cross the street, but without her consent or permission, you'd be depriving her of her self-worth."

I squared my shoulders toward him. "I would like your help. It's me asking, not anyone else."

"Very well," he said, nodding. "Sit here for a moment. I'd like to consult a colleague of mine before we go any further."

Mark stood up easily and went into the house through the door to the right of the TV. I waited for him for what seemed like an eternity. All the repetitive thoughts and longings for my ex-girlfriend were still there, but I also felt something different. There was a special energy in this place, a calmness and balance, despite the fact that the garage was a mess.

The gray concrete floor was stained in places with oil and paint, plastic storage containers and boxes and duffel bags spilled from the metal shelves, and only a small space on the worktable was clear enough for Mark to use. The smells from the tinctures and mixtures he was making were pungent and strong. Yet even with the chaos, I felt safe here. My anger slowly retreated like a snake back into its den. Mark seemed intent on helping me understand without making me feel small, and if he didn't agree to help me, I didn't know what I'd do.

Finally, Mark reappeared in the doorway and sat down beside me on the couch. "Know this, Alex: It's a great risk for me—or anyone for that matter—to take another under their care toward recovery. Especially someone who's suffering as much as you are."

A chill ran up my spine. Was it *that* obvious? Of course, my father had probably briefed Mark on what he'd seen in the last several weeks. But it wasn't just that. I was certain that Mark wasn't pitying me in the way everyone else seemed to. His grayish-brown eyes were clear and soft. He took this seriously, and I sensed that he knew my suffering as well as I did. Maybe better than I did.

Mark continued. "I consulted with my mentor, Maria, and she agrees that I should help you. But you have a choice to make, and I want you to make it with your eyes wide open. You can return to your life as it is. Eventually you'll get over this ex-girlfriend, or get back together with her, and forget about this whole summer. And your life will go on as normal."

I considered what "normal" was for me and internally rattled off a list of outward achievements: I was on track to graduate with honors, I was a pretty good tennis player, and I could build a functioning computer from scratch. I had some great friends and the drive to be successful. I was proud of all of this.

But then there was my painful attachment to Rachel. And even before Rachel, I'd always felt a deep, unmistakable sense of powerlessness in everything I did, like I was running as fast as I could over quicksand. One wrong move and I would sink, like I was sinking now. Even if I got over Rachel, I sensed that it wouldn't be too long before I got pulled down again.

"So what's the other option?" I asked.

"You find out how ignorant you truly are—how ignorant we all are. You stop looking for happiness in the external and start creating it for yourself." He began to talk with his hands, his voice gaining power. "You leave behind your poor-me attitude and take full responsibility for everything that happens to you. It's way bigger than this drama with your ex-girlfriend. You realize that any experience can be a doorway if you have the right keys."

"Okay," I answered immediately. "Whatever it takes."

He nodded. "Then I'll teach you the Process."

The Process? I had a vague memory of him talking about it before. It had something to do with what he called *magic*, but I had trouble placing it at the time.

"When do we start?" I asked.

He got up from the couch and opened the door into his house again, smiling, and swept his hand sideways as if introducing the players on a stage. "Right now."

Uncertain and exhilarated, I stepped through the door Mark held open for me.

CHAPTER 3

* * *

It's a Process

When the student is ready, the teacher will appear.

—Buddhist proverb

As I followed Mark into his living room, my eyes instantly landed on the upright piano against the left wall. A few figurines stood on it, one of them the Merlin I remembered from when Mark taught me to play. "You see, I love magic," Mark had told me all those years ago. "The world works like magic."

I remembered, then, that Mark had briefly mentioned the Process when he was teaching me to play. How it had allowed him to harness the magic of the universe for the betterment of himself and others. Maybe now, I would learn the secrets to Mark's wisdom, composure, and sharp-mindedness. I tried to contain my excitement and not get ahead of myself.

Mark said, "We'll work together for a total of three sessions, after which we'll evaluate whether the Process is appropriate for you."

"Why three?" I asked. "It's just like the three lessons it took to teach me piano."

"Good memory, nephew. That's purposeful. Things often come in threes: protons, neutrons, electrons. Id, ego, superego. Father, Son, Holy Spirit. Etcetera."

"And can you finally tell me what the Process is?"

"Of course." Mark began talking with his hands. "The Process came from a think tank of some of the greatest minds of our time, including Nobel Prize laureates, movie directors, great scientists, scholars, and psychotherapists. They wanted to compile knowledge that demonstrated how the world works, how the mind works." He paused, giving me a chance to digest his words. "In short, this is what they found: The world is an illusion, it works by magic, and the magic is perception. And if you change the way you perceive, you change the way the world works around you. In other words, you change reality."

I looked at him, my mouth starting to open. My uncle was appearing a lot like the figure of Merlin on the piano. I wanted to know more.

"How did you get started in the Process?" I asked.

He clapped a hand to my shoulder. "All in due time, nephew. First, you need to meditate."

Mark walked me to a small spare bedroom and asked me to lie down on the full-sized bed. He sat to my right near the foot of the bed and looked down at his clasped hands. A heaviness seemed to overtake him.

He spoke softly, borrowing from Frank Herbert's 1965 science fiction novel *Dune*: "A beginning is a very delicate time, Alex. The way we set things up will greatly influence the end result. If the ground rules are set improperly, the outcome may be flawed. Shifting gears later will be difficult."

I was starting to grasp the gravity of the situation. Mark was willingly taking on responsibility for me when he wasn't at all obligated to. Why was he helping me? Why was he devoting his Saturday to this? I began to feel deeply appreciative toward him.

He continued. "Before we begin, you need to be sane. You're insane right now."

I cocked my head. "Why do you think I'm *insane*?"

"You're agitated. In order for us to address your issues, I need you to be balanced. The most important step in creating balance is meditation. This is the first Tool."

"Is that like, *Ommmm*?" I closed my eyes and theatrically touched my index fingers and thumbs together.

Mark wasn't fazed. "Stop all that," he said firmly. "Lie back down with your ankles uncrossed and put your hands wherever they're comfortable. I'm going to lead you in a meditation."

His voice grew slower as he spoke:

Allow your eyes to close. Breathe slowly and deeply. Tune in to the sounds in the room and breathe in. As you breathe out, let the sounds go. They will come back. Just breathe out and let them go.

Thoughts will come into your mind. Don't fight them. Breathe out and let them go. Acknowledge the sounds and the thoughts, and then let them go. Back and forth. Back and forth. Think of the nature of ocean waves: They come in, they go out, come in, go out . . .

I don't know how much time passed while I was lying there. But eventually, Mark told me to slowly let my consciousness come back to the room. I wiggled my fingers and toes. Then he told me to sit up, straighten my arms above my head, smile, and open my eyes.

"How do you feel?" Mark asked.

Unfortunately, my mind was still racing, even after the meditation. But I noticed that I didn't feel nauseous for the first time all day. I told Mark this, and he nodded.

"Meditation is one Tool to help you get balanced. And balance is key to the Process."

* * *

I returned to Mark's house on Wednesday the next week for our second lesson. He told me that according to the Process, Saturday is the day when the universe's energy is the greatest, and Wednesday is the day it's the weakest. Wednesdays are designed to de-stress, and Saturdays are designed for connecting deeply with Source.

At the start of our second session, we sat down on the couch in his garage. Two tall glasses with a bright-green liquid in them were on the coffee table.

"Alex, there are three Tools that can help bring you into

balance. We practiced the first already: meditation. The second is drinking wheatgrass, and the third is walking."

"Wheatgrass and walking," I repeated. I was surprised at how quickly I was adjusting to this routine. After meditating daily since Saturday, I was beginning to see more results than I had after three weeks of therapy. I'd even witnessed my mind go quiet for a few seconds at a time, and I wanted more. "Is there a certain order I should use these Tools in?"

"It would be helpful if you took some wheatgrass an hour before our meetings. 'Materials first' is our motto: Take your wheatgrass and then meditate."

"Why wheatgrass?"

"It helps make your body alkaline. In an acidic state, you're out of balance. The more balanced we are, the better we can see, the better we can heal ourselves, the better decisions we make, all leading to a more satisfying life. Here, drink this. It's best to do it all at once."

He grabbed the two glasses and gave one to me. I downed it quickly.

"Blegh!" I blurted. It tasted just like liquefied grass or like a salad without any toppings.

"Tastes like balance to me!" Mark chuckled. "Now for walking. If you walk before meditation, you drain any extra adrenaline that may interfere with your practice. If you walk after, you can more deeply appreciate nature and the world. Come on, let's go."

Mark and I walked through his neighborhood side by side. The day was hot and muggy, but at times I felt like I was floating along the cream-colored sidewalk. Mark pointed out a flock of roseate spoonbills flying above us, though they looked like flamingos to me, and we stopped to admire some flowers in people's yards. But for most of the walk, he was silent, and I tried to be silent too.

"Consider walking to be a form of meditation," he said as we neared his home. "You can meditate wherever you are—on a walk, in bed, while you're eating. Thoughts will come. You may think about how hot it is, or how sweaty you are, or how bored. But choose to let every thought go as quickly as it comes. Pay attention to the sounds and your surroundings."

By the time we made it back to his garage, I realized I hadn't thought of Rachel once for the whole walk. That to me was progress.

We went into the kitchen, and Mark poured us both glasses of water. "Wheatgrass, meditation, walking. These are the easy Tools. We even use enemas to clear our minds, but I'll spare you that for now."

I gagged. "Gross."

"What's gross is having that crap stuck in your body! Better out than in, I always say." He laughed, then drank the whole glass of water in one big swig. He continued, "The purpose of these Tools is to get you sane, and that's something you lack."

I couldn't help but roll my eyes. How many times was he going to hammer that in? I didn't feel insane. I was just in a bad space. It was too strong of a word for what I was going through.

"I'm not insane, Mark." I tried to say so with certainty, but it came out sounding whiny. I knew that didn't help my case.

"I choose my words carefully," Mark said. "Many people get offended when I tell them this. They think insanity only describes people in institutions. But we have to be precise with our words. I define sanity as the ability to think in a rational and reasonable manner." He raised an eyebrow. "Have you been thinking rationally?"

"No."

"Therefore, you're insane. So are most people. The crazy thing is that people *think* they're sane. They believe their dramas are the truth. By following the Process and using the Tools, you'll see how harmful that belief is. Once we can think rationally, we can begin to change."

"I think I'm getting it."

"Good. Now go meditate."

I went into the spare bedroom and lay down on the bed, this time without Mark beside me. I focused on my breathing and the sounds in the room. After a while, thoughts of Rachel overwhelmed me. The memories made my stomach churn.

I sat up and turned left to face the vanity mirror on the dresser. I tugged at my T-shirt, ran my hands over my hairless chin and cheeks, pulled at my mop of brown hair. No matter what I did, all I saw was a thin, pale, sad kid. I turned away from the mirror and tried to continue meditating, but it was all too much—thoughts of Rachel, of my own shortcomings, of my supposed insanity. What must have been minutes felt like hours.

Finally, there was a gentle knock on the door before Mark's head poked in. "Alex, how do you feel?"

"Terrible." My voice sounded like someone else's. "I miss Rachel, and I feel like crap." I was horrified to hear myself start sobbing, but I couldn't control it. It poured out of me like water from an open fire hydrant.

Mark paused for a moment. And then, with one hand still on the doorknob, he began to laugh. Gentle, knowing laughs.

My brow tensed. "Why are you laughing?"

"I'm laughing at this drama you're performing. Are you trying to impress me?" Still smiling widely, he walked into the room and sat on the bed next to me. "Crying in itself is not inappropriate. But in doing so, you're putting on a poor-me act in order to garner sympathy. How does it serve you?"

I put my head between my knees. "I don't know. I just feel really bad."

"Precisely. You're making yourself feel bad, thus the drama. Why do you think you feel nauseous?"

"I have no clue."

His eyes narrowed. "Really?"

"I'm just sick of all this."

"Sick of what?"

After thinking hard, I finally said, "I don't know."

"Then keep meditating. I'll be back in an hour." Mark got up and soundlessly closed the door behind him.

This time, I committed to the Tool. If Mark wanted me to find my own peace, to figure out my own problems, then that's what I was going to do.

I noted the sounds in the room: ticking alarm clock on the side table, whir of the air conditioner from the ceiling vent, the birds getting louder and then quieter as they flew around outside. After a while, I could even hear my own heartbeat. It sounded weak and muted, but I listened to it anyway. Thoughts of Rachel would come, and I'd let them go. Eventually, after enough time had passed, I could feel my heart as clearly as I heard the clock tick.

Mark came in and leaned against the dresser.

"How was your meditation?"

"Better, actually."

"I can tell. So, Alex. What are you sick of?"

I surprised myself with how quickly I could now find the answer. I responded, "I'm sick of myself."

Mark smiled. "Exactly. Sick of the drama, sick of being stuck in your mind. Good. Always remember, materials first: wheatgrass, meditation, walking."

* * *

The next Saturday morning, in my dad's kitchen, I dumped a scoop of bright-green powder into a small glass and added water. I stirred it and then took the wheatgrass shot. It didn't go down easier this time, but at least I was prepared for the taste of a fresh-cut lawn. I hoped eventually I'd get used to it.

Then I went on a long walk, the sun hot on my skin. The air was so humid it felt like I was swimming down the street. But none of it bothered me. As I walked, I imagined the layers of my old self peeling off me like the sweat that dripped down my skin. I felt I was on a righteous path. With these new Tools at my disposal, I was confident that life would open its arms to me in every way.

On the drive to Mark's house for our third session, I blasted Metallica and Pearl Jam, windows down, salty air filling my lungs. Nothing was on my mind except what our third lesson would bring.

I strode into the garage, plopped down on the couch, and crossed my feet on the coffee table. Mark was watching a crime show on TV. I grabbed his can of Diet Coke from the table and took a sip.

"Hello to you too," he said.

"Mark, thank you for introducing me to the Process. I've learned so much. I'm hardly sick at all anymore. And I feel so alive—"

He interrupted me: "I appreciate your enthusiasm, but be careful. You're starting to get out of balance. You never want to be too low or too high. Staying too low or too high creates adrenaline, moving you toward insanity. Doing so puts you at risk for making poor decisions and creating more suffering for yourself and others."

I thought for a minute. "So it's like, what goes up . . . ?"

"That's right."

I understood where he was coming from. But I thought that if I could feel like this, for most of the time, for the rest of my life, I'd be unstoppable. I'd really help people, date someone who wanted me, succeed at whatever I tried—I'd do so much good, for myself and others.

Before I could argue with him, Mark said, "You seem uncertain. Meditate on this."

I went to the spare bedroom and began my grounding meditation. I focused on my breath, working with images as they surfaced: a yellow light behind my eyelids, a red ball of anger in my chest. As I slowly came down from that morning's high, I started to feel the energy coursing through my body whenever a word or image was in alignment with my intention to feel at peace. It made my veins feel like highways for energy to travel along.

Mark came into the room after I'd meditated for about forty minutes, and I asked him what this sensation was.

"When you're in balance, you'll feel open, loving, courageous, and compassionate."

"I can feel it throughout my entire body. I can even sense it moving up and down." I looked at my hands and arms as if for the first time. "I've never felt this before."

"You've probably felt it before but didn't know what it was. Or you were so preoccupied with your dramas that you missed it."

I opened and closed my hands a few times. My awareness of the energy was subsiding as I talked to Mark. "It felt so good."

"You're beginning to build trust with yourself. From a neuroscience perspective, your brain is creating new pathways and strengthening long dormant ones. And the more you make these connections, the stronger they'll become."

"Neurons that fire together, wire together," I said.

"Now, aren't you smart, Alex." He smirked, clearly aware that I was trying to impress him. He leaned his hands on his thighs and stood up. "Come on, let's go have some tea."

Mark asked me to go sit on the back porch while he made the tea, so I sat down at the outdoor table beside the pool. The sun was behind me, and everything had a hazy glow to it.

Mark came outside, set two white mugs on the table, and sat in the chair next to mine.

"Have you heard of the 'Hero's Journey'?" he asked.

I shook my head.

"Joseph Campbell was an American professor, writer, and orator best known for his work in the fields of comparative mythology. He found that many Western myths and epics follow a similar story arc. Whether it be *Star Wars*, Homer's epics, Hercules, or what have you, countless stories follow the arc of the Hero's Journey. Your life is no different."

My life is no different? That made me want to curl up on the ground. I'd been nearly knocked off course by an indifferent girlfriend. When I wasn't with Mark, I was lost in obsessive thoughts and hardly able to do anything. Suddenly, the blind optimism I'd clung to that morning evaporated.

"I don't feel like a hero," I said.

Mark gesticulated while he talked. "But you are! In your Hero's Journey, you've already begun your call to adventure. You're heading into the unknown. You're bound to receive help along your journey, like the help I'm offering you. And at some point, you may have to complete the journey on your own. My hope is that I can teach you what you need to know, so you don't have to go through what I did to override my programming. But *que sera, sera*."

"What does that mean?"

"It means whatever will be, will be."

We were silent for a while. The only sounds were the cicadas buzzing around us and a plane flying overhead.

"You have a long way to go," Mark said finally. "You've been put into a cage for your whole life. First, you took what your parents told you as the truth. Then it was your teachers, your friends, your professors, and your boss. At some point, you must learn to define yourself and your reality by and through you, and no one else."

I nodded, taking a sip of mint tea. I reflected on my past, how so many influences had shaped who I was. Mark continued: "Alex, what do you think is the greatest gift you can give a child?"

I thought for a moment. My father and mother came to mind. My father was warm, kind, and loving, and he'd raised me to be the same. He had been my steady hand through so many storms—not just now but throughout my life. For a stretch of time, he'd raised me on his own, quietly shouldering every responsibility without complaint while my mother was often absent and distant. I thought of the days in my childhood I'd spent wishing she would come home, that I could see her again, after she left on one of her grand expeditions. Wondering where she was. My heart clenched.

"Easy," I said. "The greatest gift is love."

"Wrong. Love can be part of it, but it's not the main element." Mark leaned forward in his chair, his eyes full of life. "The greatest thing you can give a child, or anyone for that matter, is independence. When a person has independence, they can make their own world. They're not dependent on you or anyone else. If you give a child independence, you've helped them achieve freedom. That is my hope with you. When you must face your demons alone, without me, you'll be ready. You will become your own master."

"If you give a man a fish . . ."

Mark smirked. "You do like your quotes, don't you?"

* * *

It had gotten dark as we talked. We'd lit a citronella candle and put on bug spray to survive the mosquitoes. Mark was smoking a cigar, and thick clouds of smoke played in the lamplight when he exhaled. The smell was somehow comforting.

I knew my three sessions of the Process were up. I was afraid to hear Mark's verdict as to whether or not we'd continue training. I wanted more. I wanted to learn everything, to become a master like him. Finally, I'd found someone who made the spiritual teachings from books and videos come to life. He was wise, fearless, and compassionate. Even with all my dramas and imperfections, he understood me. He saw me for me.

I took a deep breath, bracing myself for disappointment. "Mark, can we continue working together?"

"Yes," he responded without hesitation. "You still have a long way to go, bub."

Relief rushed through me. Still, I wondered why he was making this huge commitment. It couldn't just be out of the kindness of his heart. Could it?

I straightened up in my chair. "So how do you want me to pay for training?"

"Give me a million dollars when you make your first five million." He smirked.

One *million* dollars? Fine. Whatever it took. "I'll do my best," I said earnestly.

He laughed, throwing his head back. "Alex, don't worry about it. I'm not doing this for profit or what I can get out of it. In fact, I hate to burst your bubble, but I do everything for myself."

"What do you mean?"

"I do it because I know this secret: By making the world around me better, I make my life better. So by helping you, I know I'll reap rewards too."

"That's a funny way of looking at it," I said.

"Perhaps. But there is one catch: You must always earn what you get. Otherwise, you'll experience a short circuit."

"A short circuit?"

"You'll suffer in some form or another. Ever wonder why lottery winners or famous athletes tend to lose all their money?"

"Because they spend it on stupid things?" I said, only half joking.

"Because they haven't earned it." He took a puff of his cigar, and smoke curled out as he spoke. "The universe always finds a way to balance itself. What you don't earn, the universe restores back to the status quo."

"Kinda like karma?"

"Be careful not to mix metaphors, Alex. It can make things confusing. Just remember that if you did not earn it, it will be taken right back from you. That's why I'll leave it to you to earn your training."

I nodded. "I'll find a way to pay you back."

"You don't listen well. I don't want your money, nephew! I want you to earn what you get. The right thing will come. Trust the universe."

"At least let me wash your car. You know, wax on, wax off?"

Mark just laughed in response, free and easy like a child would, not holding back.

CHAPTER 4

* * *

Fear Is the Mind Killer

Without change, something sleeps inside us, and seldom awakens. The sleeper must awaken.

—Paul Atreides, *Dune* (1984 film)

I went back to UCF for the fall semester of my senior year feeling like a new man. My nausea had all but subsided. I felt healthy and well rested. I'd saved up some money working over the summer. The Tools and the Process had consistently improved my mind and my life, and Mark's influence was evident in everything I did. Rachel still crossed my mind every so often, but I felt I was finally through the worst of it and ready to be open to whatever the year would bring me.

One night a few weeks into the semester, I went to study at the café in the student center. I ordered a latte at the counter, then started unpacking my things at a table against the wall.

The next time I looked up, I saw Rachel walking toward the counter. She was wearing denim cutoffs, a black short-sleeve shirt, and white sneakers. Her tan had deepened over the summer, and her dark hair was falling past her shoulders rather than being up in the usual ponytail.

It felt like my heart was caught in my throat. I willed myself to remember the Tools. I tried to pay attention to the sounds around me, but they were overwhelming. The roaring coffee grinder, the screech of the milk steamer, and the college-kid racket all made it impossible to focus. I raced to pack up so I could take a walk to clear my head, hopefully before Rachel noticed me.

"Alex! Your latte's ready," the barista called from the counter.

Shit.

I took hesitant steps toward the counter. When Rachel saw me, her eyes widened before she regained composure and smiled. I smiled back, conscious of the beads of sweat bubbling up on my neck and the slight dizziness in my head. I walked up to the counter as casually as I could, but I felt like the Tin Man from Oz before he was oiled.

After I grabbed my coffee, Rachel stepped toward me and gave me a hug.

"Hey, Rachel," I managed to say.

"Hey, Alex. Should we talk?"

* * *

We stepped outside the student center and walked toward a table where it would be quieter. Coincidentally, it was also more romantic. String lights crisscrossed the open courtyard, and the surrounding hedgerows formed a wall around us. Part of me still wanted to run away. I thought I was in control of myself, but at the first sight of her, I could feel every ounce of self-control evaporating within me like my training had just flown out the window.

I remembered something Mark had told me when I was telling him about my nausea. I was throwing up a few days a week, and sometimes I even forced myself to throw up to relieve the nausea. One time it got so bad, I became extremely dehydrated and had to be hospitalized.

"The nausea is telling you something is wrong," Mark had said simply.

"Could it be Rachel?"

"She could be a trigger, Alex, but remember everything is happening in your head. She's just a representation of something that's in your mind."

"Like that perception stuff you told me about."

"Yes, your world works by how you perceive it. Change that, and you change your world. Magic."

"I remember."

"At the same time, you need to learn to listen more deeply to your body. And apparently, your body is telling you something."

"So, what do I do?"

"Start by understanding all of this is happening in your mind. Create some separation from becoming so absorbed in this fear. Take some steps to create joy in your world. And most importantly, you're in college. Enjoy your life! Continuing to obsess and worry will create more worry, since that's what you are focusing your attention on. What you focus on, you create more of. Simple."

What you focus on, you create more of. That seemed especially important now, as I sat across from Rachel.

Obviously, on the one hand, Mark's advice was to separate myself from Rachel and all the dramas we got caught in. But another part of me was curious whether the circumstances had changed. Maybe things *could* be better between us if that's what I focused on. I had the Process now. I felt balanced. (Usually.) And if I could create my own reality, couldn't I create ours?

Finding a quiet spot, we sat down across from one another at one of the wrought-iron tables.

"Hope I didn't mess up your study session," Rachel said.

"Not at all. You're a welcome distraction."

"Happy I could save you, then." She grinned almost girlishly, looking me over slowly. "I can't put my finger on it. Did something happen to you this summer? You seem . . . calmer than usual."

I laughed. "I've been meditating, putting in the effort, making plans for myself. I've grown a lot. I'm glad you can tell."

She took a sip of coffee, keeping her eyes on me. The

energy between us felt charged, like we were on the precipice of something. Her eyes betrayed her. She seemed interested in me.

"Well, I like what I see. Looks like you took my advice to heart."

The way she was looking at me, the certainty I felt about us . . . The moment felt right. I knew this could work, and all I had to do was take that initiative she needed me to.

I couldn't stop myself—the words poured out of me. "I did take your advice. And I did it for you. I want you back, Rachel."

I shouldn't have said it. Instantly, the energy dropped between us. She looked at me almost sadly, shaking her head like a disappointed parent.

"You know, I did a lot of thinking over the summer. I thought about us a lot, about all the times we'd taken breaks before this. Can I be honest?"

I nodded, bracing myself.

She shaped out the words with her hands. "When we're dating, I feel like I have a puppy. You're cute, kind, and always happy to see me. But I feel like you're something to take care of rather than a partner to take on life with."

A puppy? A *puppy*? If our breakup conversation had felt like a flaming arrow through my chest, this was the whole quiver. My entire being begged to sink through the chair, past the cobblestones, through the dirt, straight into the core of the earth.

"You know, you're not easy to be with either." I was

surprised by the quickness of my anger. "You're distant, cold. Nothing's ever enough for you. Not my culture, not my affection, nothing."

Her expression was blank. "You know what? You're right. None of it's enough for me. I'm sorry, but it's true."

After shouldering her purse, Rachel grabbed her coffee and stood up. "Bye, Alex. Maybe I'll see you around." I watched her walk away and turn right down the narrow street.

Out of the corner of my eye, I saw a couple at a nearby table glancing at me and whispering to each other. Hot shame ran through my body, even while I was still trembling with anger. I knew that I had failed. I'd failed myself, I'd failed Rachel, and I'd failed Mark. *I've grown a lot*, I had said to her. *Grown a lot. What a joke.*

* * *

During my 7:30 AM class the next day, the balding professor's voice droned on and on. I drummed my pencil on the desk, tapped my foot uncontrollably. The lesson was something about embedded systems design, but I couldn't will myself to care. The rage was back, and this time I knew I was the one to blame for it.

For the first time in my life, I left in the middle of class. I walked aimlessly around campus for hours, ignoring the sunburn on my face and the sweat soaking my shirt.

The next morning, I stayed in bed till noon. Even worse, I didn't go to any of my classes for several days. I didn't even study. I just lay around, watched TV, and nibbled on protein bars and potato chips. My appetite was gone again, and I missed an exam or maybe even two—I wasn't keeping up with the syllabi, so I couldn't know.

After a week of this, I looked around my apartment living room. There was nothing decorating the white walls. Half-eaten bags of chips and crushed beer cans littered the coffee table and floor. The black futon cushion, which had been scratched to bits by a previous roommate's cat, was dusted with crumbs and salt. I hadn't changed out of my gray sweatshirt and sweatpants since the day before.

To make matters worse, I knew I'd brought all of this onto myself. I began to see how right Mark was—I was responsible for this. I'd let myself get insane, as Mark would say. I'd given up on the Tools, and now look at me. With one conversation, almost two months of training were chalked up to nothing. I was right back where I was before I even knew about the Process.

I started crying in a reckless way. I needed help, but I didn't want Mark to know I'd abandoned his teachings so quickly. So I called my friend Dan, an alumnus and mentor who always gave solid advice. I told him what I'd been mulling over since that night at the student center café: I wanted to take a semester off.

"Alex, whatever decision you make will end up being the

right one," he replied. "I believe in you, and I know you'll finish college at some point."

That was it, then. After I thanked him and got off the phone, I threw open my suitcase and started stuffing my clothes into it.

* * *

I declared a leave of absence from college in early October and arrived back at my parents' house on a Saturday afternoon. My father and Elisabeth were in the kitchen shaping out meatballs for dinner that night. When I let them know about my decision, Elisabeth looked surprised, but my father's face fell.

"Absolutely not." My dad's voice, usually soft and gentle, boomed at me.

"It's already done," I said. "I'll keep working with Mark. I won't waste my time."

He scoffed. "What if you never go back? What will you do then? How will you qualify for a good job?"

"I'll go back, I promise."

He took a deep breath and leaned forward on the counter. "I can't force you to do anything. But just know that you don't become successful in life by taking the easy way out."

"The easy way? Dad . . ."

He held up a hand, pieces of meat stuck to it. "We'll talk later, Alexander."

I stomped into my room and chucked my bags on the bed. I wasn't going to bother unpacking yet. I just needed to get out of the house, away from everyone's disappointment. *Still the kid throwing toys around*, I thought.

* * *

As I pulled up to Mark's house the next day, I found him and Nice working in the front garden. They were planting flowers of all colors in heaps of dark, fresh dirt. Nice was wearing tan Bermuda shorts and a short-sleeve button-up shirt. Mark's wide-brimmed sun hat made him look like a tourist, and his face was misty and flushed with the heat. I accidentally slammed my car door on the way out.

"What're you doing here?" Mark called when he saw me, holding a hand up to his eyes.

"I'm taking a semester off."

"Why? I gave you the Tools. What's the problem?"

"You did. I just need to get over this thing with Rachel. For real this time."

"Alex, you're in spiritual bypass." He threw his spade to the ground and started taking off his thick work gloves.

"What?"

"Spiritual bypass. You're using spiritual ideas and practices to avoid facing your emotional issues. In other words, you're avoiding real life because you think that's safer. You're using the Process as a crutch."

I hung my head and toed at the grass.

"You should go back," he said. "You don't get anywhere running from your fears."

"Take it easy on the kid," Nice said, leaning back on her heels and swiping her brow with the back of her hand. "You're too hard on him."

"Nothing close to how hard my mentor was on me," Mark muttered. "*Man*, Ed really nailed me. But that was the only way I could learn. And the same goes for Alex."

"I don't mind," I said. "I like that he's hard on me."

Nice smiled, then pointed to her right. "Alex, could you grab that thing of fertilizer for me please?"

I assumed she was trying to change the subject. I grabbed the green Miracle-Gro container and walked it over to her.

"Listen," Mark said, standing up with ease, dropping his more confronting demeanor. "Whatever decision you make will end up being the right one. That's the way the universe works."

Relief filled my body. "That's exactly what my friend said, who helped me make the decision to leave!"

"Well, perhaps it's a synchronicity."

Mark must have seen my apparent confusion, for he went on to explain, "Synchronicity involves meaningful coincidences. Events that are surprisingly connected. Pay attention to these moments, as it's often the universe trying to tell you something. In other words, there are no accidents. Everything happens for a reason and purpose."

"Is it a sign? A message?"

"There you go again with your New Age stuff." He chuckled. "Just listen to what the world is telling you. Have you been using the Tools?"

"I was, until about a week ago."

"There you go. To be honest, I think you should go back. You reek of fear. But you have the freedom to make your own decisions, and that freedom is imperative."

"If I stay, will you keep training me?" I asked.

"Depends. Are you still insane?"

I smiled. "Yes, Mark. I'm insane."

"Good. Maybe now we can get somewhere."

* * *

I decided to spend the night at Mark's house. I didn't feel ready to go home and face my father's concern again. I'd let him down enough in the past few months, and it felt like there was nothing I could say to patch things up.

Mark suggested we watch *Dune*, the 1980s movie in which Kyle MacLachlan plays a young prince named Paul Atreides. The three of us—Mark, Nice, and me—munched on buttery popcorn in big red bowls together on the living room couch as we watched the movie on their large, boxy TV. The woman who introduced the movie said something similar to what Mark had told me during our first session, about how important a beginning is.

"This is a teaching movie for the Process," Mark said. "So pay attention to the message."

"The special effects are a bit old-school for my taste," Nice said, winking at me.

She was right. In one of the first scenes, Paul and an advisor spar with each other, using these blocky cartoon shields to protect themselves. It looked ridiculous, but I kept in mind what Mark had told me.

When the Reverend Mother was about to test Paul with something called a *pain amplifier*, Mark instructed me to pay close attention. The pain amplifier was a device, a box, that simulated pain without doing actual harm. If Paul removed his hand from the pain amplifier, the Reverend Mother would pierce him with a poison needle and kill him. She said a true human would realize that pain was an illusion and not remove his hand. Only an animal would blindly react to the pain. Paul succeeded, enduring great pain but maintaining enough control to keep his hand in the box.

I felt a pang of recognition, remembering Mark comparing me to a dog in a locked room—and the puppy Rachel accused me of being. I was obviously more animal than human. Given the chance, I'd have taken out my hand at the first opportunity.

I looked away from the screen toward Mark, reclining in his seat on the couch. Sometimes I felt he was more human than I could ever be. More fearless. More successful. He had faith where I had doubt, and knowledge where I had fear. He could wield magic. What could I do?

Then I remembered a story Mark had told me. He and his daughter, when she was very young, were having dinner around a campfire after a hike when storm clouds began to roll in. He asked her if she wanted to make the rain clouds go away, and she said, "Yes, Daddy, let's stop the rain!" They both raised their hands in the air and imagined the clouds dissipating, and sure enough, they watched as the clouds separated and blew away. It worked about four more times after that too. Then, when they finally climbed into the tent that night, it started to rain.

"Did you make that happen too?" I'd asked Mark in amazement.

"Who knows?" he'd replied.

That question reverberated in my head now—who knows? *Who knows*? Mark didn't know what he could be until he mastered the Process. I had no clue what I could be outside of this obsession with Rachel. Maybe I could banish the storm clouds from my own life. I wondered who I'd be then. *Who knows?* But I'd never know until I raised up my hands and tried.

After the movie ended and Mark and Nice had gone to bed, I replayed the pain amplifier scene in my head at least a dozen times. Paul's words rang in my ears: *Fear is the mind killer . . . Fear is the mind killer.* I'd never heard that idea put so well.

"Fear is the mind killer," I whispered to myself. "Where the fear has gone there will be nothing. Only I will remain." *Only I will remain. Only I will remain.*

I stretched out on the couch, put an elbow behind my head, and fell into the deepest sleep I'd had in weeks.

* * *

The next morning, Mark gently shook me awake to tell me breakfast was ready. I went into the dining room and found plates of blueberry pancakes, scrambled eggs, dry toast, and golden hash browns on the table. Mark brought in three glasses of wheatgrass from the kitchen, which we all drank first before eating.

Mark and Nice were both wearing white bathrobes, sitting at the table like hotel guests who ordered room service. They talked easily and freely about their weeks. They picked at each other. I noticed each leaned in whenever the other spoke.

Then Nice turned to me, her hands folded under her chin. "So what did your father say about you taking a break from school?"

"He's pretty against it," I said. "So is the rest of the family. And some of my friends say I'm being stupid."

"They don't exist," Mark said with a shrug, as if his meaning were perfectly clear.

Nice laughed. "Here we go."

"What do you mean they don't exist?" I asked.

"For any individual, everyone else is a mirror," Mark began. "So whenever people talk, no matter what they're saying, it always reflects back on themselves. In their world, only they exist. They're coming from their experiences and their perceptions. So to take the things they say personally would be . . ."

"Nonsense."

"Exactly. Put another way, other people's behavior has nothing to do with you. In their world, they're playing out their own pain and suffering. Everyone speaks for themselves." Mark smiled. "For example, my mom loved to guilt-trip me. But when I realized it wasn't about me, I stopped playing into it."

"How'd you manage that?" I asked.

"My mom would start giving me a guilt trip, and I would softly and without reactivity let her know she was doing guilt. Or I would use humor to try to snap her out of her insane state. The key is to not get dragged into it." Mark paused briefly, then elaborated: "It takes two: the guilt tripper and the victim. Don't let yourself be a victim. Let it fall off you. Eventually, the guilt tripper will run out of fuel and see it isn't working on you, and that will be the end of the guilt trip."

"Okay, that makes sense."

"Another example. A few years ago, it was my birthday, and my son didn't call or send a card," Mark said.

"What? That's terrible. You must've been mad."

"Why would I be?" Mark looked puzzled. "It wasn't about me."

"But it's inconsiderate. He's your kid. He should show respect."

"You sound like your father."

I laughed. "You're right, I do."

"I love my children," Mark explained. "Under no circumstances would I want them to feel bad on account of me. The beautiful thing is the day after my birthday, my son came to see me with cards, hugs and kisses, and an apology. The apology I could do without. I'm just happy my kids are happy."

"That's powerful, Mark."

"Everyone is a mirror," he replied. "So why do you care so much about what other people say?"

I thought for a moment. "I guess I'm afraid they're right. That I'll never go back to college, or I won't succeed, even if I do."

"Aha!" Mark took a quick bite of his toast. "What did you think of *Dune*?"

"I loved it."

"Do you remember Paul's mantra? The one he repeated whenever he faced fear?"

I nodded and repeated the whole mantra word for word. For the first time, I saw Mark's eyes widen in surprise. A rush of pride flowed through me.

"Excellent, Alex! Fear is an illusion. When you actually face it, you realize it was not as you initially perceived. You must take control of it and use it for growth, not let it destroy you. It's an emotion that's there to tell you something—to get you to take action."

"But how do you take action when you're in pain?" I asked.

"You can only master what's painful!" Mark boomed. "Think of how a sword is shaped by fire. The fire melts the blade, and the blacksmith refines it until it's sharp and ready for battle. So goes your pain. It's here to shape you, to mold you. So use it."

"I want to learn how," I said.

"Remember the box Paul put his hand into? The pain amplifier? You're in one right now, Alex." He pointed at me. "Only your box is fear. It's an illusion, and you know it. But you must hold still to let the fear pass through you, not react."

I remembered the final words of Paul's monologue: *And then only I will remain.*

"But who's testing me?" I asked. "Who's holding the needle?"

"Who do you think?" Mark laughed.

* * *

For most of the morning, I did odd jobs for Mark. In the afternoon, Mark had me wash his glassware while he made fresh herbal remedies and supplements for the week. He swore by these concoctions and claimed they eased anything from a hangover to the flu. For as long as I'd known him, I wasn't sure I'd ever seen him sick, so maybe he was right.

I stood over the metal sink against the side wall in the garage, cleaning vials and jars with brushes and soap. Bits of crushed herbs, powders, and oily liquids swirled down the drain when I rinsed.

At a wooden worktable to my left, Mark had large jars filled with all kinds of herbs—chamomile, mullein, rose hip, turmeric, ginger. He'd dip a wooden spoon into the powders and pick up the dried herbs with his fingers, mixing them in what looked like jam jars. He didn't use a scale or seem to measure anything.

Suddenly, Mark turned to me and said, "You saw Rachel while you were there." It wasn't a question.

My shoulders tensed up. "I did."

"What did you two talk about?"

"I don't want to get into it."

"Alex," he said sternly.

"All right, I caved. I tried to get her back, but she rejected me all over again."

"I don't understand why you put yourself down for her," he said. "You're allowing your self-worth to be a function of whether she wants to be with you or not. So what?"

I set down the large mason jar I was holding. "So *what*? I love her so much it hurts. What can I do about that?"

"You're telling me that if a beautiful girl came here, wanting you, your feelings for Rachel would stay the same?"

"Of course they would."

"Really think about that for a moment."

I did as Mark asked. I imagined a beautiful woman waltzing right into that very garage. I pictured her kissing me passionately, telling me how much she wanted to be with me, how much she liked my eyes and my mind. It was no surprise that my mood quickly improved.

"Okay, maybe not," I admitted.

"Alex, you've been *abused* since the day you were born."

Did he just say "abused"? That I'd been abused? I cocked my head at Mark, but he kept on working like he'd only commented on the weather.

I shook my head. "Abused? No, I haven't. I had a pretty good childhood. In fact, I had it better than a lot of people."

"You were abused, as all of us were," he repeated. He leaned against the worktable and folded his hands in front of him. "From the second you were born, you were put in a cage. God—at that time, your parents—looked down upon you day after day, saying, 'You can't do this, you can't do that, don't touch the hot stove, you're limited.' There was always somebody smarter than you, prettier than you, faster than you, because there was always somebody older than you. So you grew up with a program saying, 'I'm not good enough.' But that's not something you can just sit there and say to yourself, so you do things to cover it up. But deep down, when things go badly and when you feel guilty, you don't think you deserve good things—because *you* aren't good. *That's* the program. That's what you're actually fighting. And it goes deeper than you know."

I suddenly felt very heavy, like there was molasses in my blood. "'Abused' is an ugly word for that. It's like 'insane.' They're both ugly words."

"Sometimes things need to be ugly for you to get it," Mark said. "This programming has nothing to do with reality. It goes on simply because you were born and you're alive. We all have this issue. Once you're aware of it, you'll see it everywhere. Go meditate on this."

"But I'm not fin—"

"The dishes can wait."

* * *

I left the light off in the spare bedroom as the midafternoon sun cast shards of light through the blinds. When I sat on the bed and closed my eyes, at first I saw nothing, thought nothing. Then my mind presented the conversation with Rachel at the café, like it was a movie. I wanted so badly to look away, but I didn't. As she spoke, I couldn't see anything in her face—not love for me, or regret, or care. Just a faraway look. Just apathy. Maybe that's all I'd ever seen there.

In my mind, I reached out to her, and she leaned away. Again and again, I moved toward her, and each time she'd lean back just enough so that I'd miss her. It felt like I was in one of those dreams where you need to run and save somebody, but the ground is sticky and holds you back. And then, I finally understood. For the rest of the meditation, I was at ease.

I went back into the garage and picked up the brush and a jar. Mark had finished with his concoctions and was at the worktable tinkering with an old portable radio.

"What did you learn?" he asked when he saw me.

"Every time I ask Rachel to take me back, I diminish myself. I make myself weaker."

Mark nodded slowly. "Good, Alex. When it comes to relationships, be careful about going back. In nearly all situations, the insanity of both partners will return time and time again—unless the couple is willing to work on themselves. A rare exception indeed. As a general rule, move on. Go and find someone in alignment with who you are now and who you wish to become."

"Thank you, Mark. I think I'd be in a ditch somewhere without you."

He held up a finger. "I don't exist."

"Then who's this guy always talking about enemas and insanity?"

We laughed together, and immediately I felt freer. How did he do it? How did he always seem to have the exact answer I needed, no matter what issue I brought to him? He was so certain. It seemed impossible.

"Mark, how do you know so much? How are you so wise?" I asked.

"I only know the Process," he said simply.

"It seems like you know more than that. So much of what you say is spot on. It's remarkable."

"I'm just a conduit, a channel."

"Do you tap into spirits? Or beings from other worlds?"

"No, this isn't *Ghostbusters*." He laughed. "The Process has trained me to look past my ego and connect to my Higher Self. This is the place where the answers come through. There is no agenda and very little thinking. What is needed appears."

"Do you think I'll ever be able to do that?" I asked.

"I'm certain of it," he responded. "But before you can, you have to face yourself fully."

"How do I do that?"

"The easiest way is to use the Tools and follow the teachings. This will naturally lead you to know yourself. But we also have something called *Intensives*. These are methods that allow you to take a deep look at everything you're not seeing in an intense and short time period."

My heart rate increased at the thought. "Maybe I could benefit from that."

"No, you wouldn't. And I hope you don't have to. I needed an extra kick in the pants to get over my programming, but maybe you won't. Seeing the dark parts within you can really mess you up if you're not prepared. If you follow the Process and use the Tools, you can do just as well."

Something in me felt that without doing an Intensive, whatever that experience might be, I'd never get to where Mark was. But I knew Mark wouldn't budge, so I let it go. Besides, I felt really good where I was at. Why mess it up?

* * *

Autumn passed quickly, though the summer heat stuck around. By the beginning of December, South Florida didn't look very different. Green palm fronds still sprouted from yards and beside highways. Birds still called. But I felt that something deep within myself had shifted.

I was playing tennis more, reading books, and working at a law firm. I made arrangements to go back to college in the spring, which relieved both my father and me. But

I wasn't just doing all of this to avoid my thoughts. In fact, I'd sat with them long enough by now that I could see them for what they were—a program that said nothing about the person I actually was.

I'd also signed up for a couple of online dating sites and connected with a woman, Joni, who lived in Miami. A few days after New Year's, I picked her up and we drove south toward the Overseas Highway, the sole thoroughfare through the Florida Keys. It was a beautiful seventy-two degrees, so we had the windows down. The sun was to our right, threatening to race to the horizon before we could reach the sunset spot she'd told me about.

We chatted and laughed the whole way down, the water stretching out for miles to either side. The narrow highway brought us past brightly colored houses, tourist traps with big signs showcasing a marlin or a mermaid or a hooked sea bass, and beaches dotted with late-afternoon sunbathers. After crossing the seven-mile bridge, we turned into a neighborhood, parked on a side street, and walked a few minutes to a small beach where about thirty people were already standing around or sitting on beach blankets. One couple had a boom box that was playing lively Latin music.

I shook out the blanket and laid it on the white sand, with the tide coming in just ten feet ahead of us. As the sun dipped down into the ocean and got swallowed up, with a slow and heartfelt song coming from the boom box, I kissed Joni. For the few minutes it lasted, I felt deeply connected to her. As I felt Rachel slip away, finally, a new energy rose up in me.

After I dropped her off and went home, Joni called. She said that being with me had inspired her to reconnect with her ex-boyfriend. I had to think that was funny. Whether or not she was being sincere, I enjoyed the irony—I'd helped her recommit to a relationship, and she'd helped me finally release one.

That night, I lay in bed with my hands behind my head. I was going back to college in just a few days, and I had to ask myself: *Would this time be different?* Just a few short months ago, in August, I'd thought I was the king of the world. I'd thought that a few hours of meditation and some good advice had fundamentally changed me. Now, I knew it wasn't that simple. I would have to keep up with the Tools and Mark's teachings, even when I got caught in the pain amplifier of my own fears.

Could I do it?

All I knew was that I was going to put my arms into the air and try.

CHAPTER 5

* * *

The Gift

Love is the one thing we're capable of perceiving that transcends dimensions of time and space. Maybe we should trust that, even if we can't understand it.

—Dr. Amelia Brand, *Interstellar* (2014 film)

Mark often sang a song from the 1960s movie *Finian's Rainbow*, "When I'm Not Near the Girl I Love." He'd move his hands like a conductor's, his eyes closed, as he swayed and sang along. In the movie, the character played by Tommy Steele finds a woman he thinks is his lover in a clearing but soon realizes that it's not her. And yet he thinks he might be able to love this woman, too, just the same.

Mark put it this way: "This isn't just about relationships. It's a way of living. Appreciate wherever you happen to be, without craving to be somewhere else. If you can do this, you'll be rewarded."

So that's what I did. I chose to love what was in front of me: morning meditations as I struggled not to nod off, the small print of textbooks about systems theory and business best practices, the fluorescent lights buzzing in the library, and evening walks. Whenever I got sucked into the pain amplifier, Mark would twirl through my head and sing, "When I'm not near the one I love . . ." and I'd remember to appreciate it, all of it, as much as I could.

After having barely made it into college in the first place, I graduated from UCF with summa cum laude honors. When we threw our graduation caps into the air, and they rained down all around us, I thought this would be my life: a series of ups and downs, joys and pains. And I could choose to either embrace them or suffer from them. I hoped I'd choose to embrace them.

After college, I went back home and took up a temporary job with a real estate agency while I prepared for law school. And for the first time in my life, I dated widely and often. There was Carmen, who played tennis with me every Wednesday; Tammy, who basically lived at the beach; and Elena, who blasted the Grateful Dead in her car. I was at my most grounded, my most centered, and women seemed to appreciate it.

For some strange reason, my potential dates would always—and I mean *always*—call right after I finished meditating at Mark's house. One day, when we were in his garage, I asked Mark why he thought this was.

"Magic," he said.

"And perception is the magic that creates the world."

"Precisely. Your energy is strong while working in the Process. You're sane. You're creating all of this."

It sounded too good to be true, but I was hard-pressed to doubt it. There really was no explanation. I meditated at different times on Wednesday and Saturday, and no matter what, the calls came in.

"So how do I know when I've met the one for me?" I asked.

Mark stood up from the couch and opened the door to the house. "When you're picking up your date, open the car door for the lady." He playfully waved his hand and took lilting steps over the threshold. "If she returns the favor to you—" He waved again from the inside, and I walked through. "Then hold on to her."

"That's it?"

"That's a big part of it."

* * *

On a Wednesday in October, a girl named Heather messaged me on an online dating site. She went to UCF, worked part-time in retail, and had a passion for art and drawing. When she told me she loved M. C. Escher, I thought she was talking about a rapper, and I wondered if she'd ever stop laughing at that. Heather loved that I played the piano and read books by Chopra and Tolle, and it seemed we could talk on the phone for hours without taking a breath.

"So when are we meeting up?" she asked while we were on the phone one night.

I was sitting on the back porch at my father's house, looking up at the stars in the black sky. "Be patient, young Padawan," I said, referring to the *Star Wars* term for aspiring Jedi knights. "All in due time."

"And why do I have to be patient?" she teased.

"I'm going to New York in a couple of weeks to see some friends. I was thinking we could hang out after that."

"Aw, Alex. You're stalling!" Her laugh was high and full of joy.

"What? No, I'm not! I just don't wanna see you once, then have to wait forever to see you again."

"We're meeting up before that," she said with certainty. "In fact, how about this weekend? Are you free on Saturday?"

I rubbed my forehead with my left hand. I'd never had a woman be so eager to meet up with me before, and maybe she was right—maybe I was stalling. But why I would stall like that, I couldn't figure out.

"And if I insist that I'd rather wait?" I said.

"Nope. Too bad. Not letting you," she responded.

"I had a feeling."

We laughed together again, my whole body feeling warm.

"Look," she began. "My grandparents live near you. So I'm gonna drive from Orlando this weekend just to stay with them and see you. And if you bail, I'll never bother you again. Deal?"

"Okay, Heather. Deal. You win this round."

"It won't be the last time!" she said.

And I had a feeling she was right.

That Saturday, while my parents were out of town for the weekend, I spent the entire day cleaning, meditating, and cooking. The menu was spaghetti with a vegetarian "meat" sauce, an Olive Garden–style salad, and French bread toasted with butter and coarse-chopped garlic. Once the preparations were made, I went to pick up Heather from her grandparents' apartment.

She came to the apartment building stairs wearing a white sundress with burgundy roses on it, and her long dark hair was in a loose ponytail. I opened the passenger door of my old Nissan Sentra for her, and she smiled as she climbed inside.

When we made it to my house, I broiled the bread in the oven and heated up the pasta sauce. Heather watched me closely, leaning on the kitchen island counter.

"A man who opens doors for me *and* cooks? I didn't know they made them like that."

"I didn't know they made women as beautiful as you."

She playfully rolled her eyes. "Easy with the cheese, Alex. Which I never thought I'd say around pasta."

Once the bread was ready, I opened the oven door and let the steam pour out before I removed the tray. I asked Heather to sit down at the dining table while I served our plates, then I sat down beside her and poured us each some red wine in big stemmed glasses.

I held up my glass. "To being here now," I said.

"To being here now." She clinked her glass against mine.

We ate together at the dining table while we watched game six of the World Series. We were both rooting for the Florida Marlins, the underdogs, to win over the Yankees. She assured me that if I wanted the Marlins to win, they would win. I admired her certainty. Between plays, we talked about everything from zodiac signs to the meaning of life.

And sure enough, the Marlins won 2–0, almost as if by magic. We leaped up from our chairs and cheered and hugged, then held each other's gazes for a while longer than friends would.

The words poured out of me. "Heather, this might sound weird, but I feel like I've known you for a long time."

"Me too," she said dreamily. "When I saw your picture online, I had a . . . feeling."

"What kind of a feeling?"

Her eyes were shining. "Like, I felt I've known you forever, or at least a really long time. And I knew we would get along really well, no matter what happened. I don't want to freak you out. I know we're just meeting each other, and I don't have wild expectations. I'm just excited to see where it goes. I'm hopeful."

My heart rate picked up. I wasn't sure I'd ever dated a woman who was so forward with her affection, and the experience of it confused me. Part of me rose up to hear her say that. To know she was here because she saw something in us. But another part of me was terrified, like if I let things go too far too fast, I could get really hurt.

"That doesn't freak me out," I said, though it was kind of a lie. "I'm hopeful too."

I poured us some more wine, and then Heather and I got settled on the couch. As the wine flowed and the bottle emptied, our shoulders leaned forward, we played with each other's hands, and our words came more slowly.

Nighttime came, and I lit a couple of candles on the coffee table. The wavy flames cast a sunset on Heather's cheek, on her full lips. Looking at her like that, my chest felt tight. Something in me was screaming that she would become important to me, but I hadn't even been dating for a year yet. Rachel still wasn't a distant memory. Was I ready for this?

Heather turned to look at me, and the candlelight lit fires in her big green eyes. The wine had softened her face. "Tell me. Why are you here, Alex Nottingham? What's your purpose on this big blue-green rock in space?"

"To make the world better, in whatever way I'm called to."

"Good answer."

"I gotta thank my uncle for that one. But, yeah. It's the truth."

She took my hand in hers and held it on her crossed legs. "So how do you want to make the world better?"

I thought for a minute, then responded, "I want to start a business. I don't want to work for anyone else. Yes, money is important, but I don't want it just to be about money. I love to be creative, passionate, and inspired. I want to make a difference and help others. And I want to have a family. That's my dream."

"I love that dream."

"What's yours?" I asked.

She smiled, looking off into space. "I want to build a great life and a great home with someone who's really my partner. I want to marry my person and start a family."

"Great minds," I said.

"Great minds," she echoed.

Silence hung between us for a few moments. Heather's eyes dropped from my eyes to my lips, and I had no choice but to lean in and kiss her. The sensation overwhelmed me, so much that I pulled back quickly. It felt like too much, even though this was just our first date. It felt like committing to someone.

Her smile was dreamy. "It feels so easy with you, just like it was talking on the phone. I was worried it wouldn't live up."

Hearing her say that made me feel like I was high. "I know. I've never dated someone I could talk to for hours without getting bored."

"Exactly. And it helps that you're a good cook. If this all had sucked"—she motioned to the empty plates and wineglasses—"you would've been in trouble."

She looked at me then with an openness that made me turn to the window, embarrassed. She slowly stood up, placed her hands on my shoulders, and leaned close to my ear. "Would you want to go look at the stars together?"

My cheeks grew hot, and I prayed she wouldn't notice. I went to get us a blanket from the hall closet. When

I returned, she was leaning against the back door, looking at me intently, and as I moved closer, she stepped aside. I opened the back door, and we walked into the humid dark together in our bare feet.

Hours passed quickly until it was time for Heather to go back to her grandparents' place. On the way to my car, she skipped down the driveway. I almost couldn't believe it when she opened up the driver's side door for me, motioning me inside like a valet. A knot formed in my throat. It was just like Mark had said. *If she returns the favor . . .*

"Your carriage, my dear," she said in a deep faux-English accent.

I shook my head as I climbed inside. "You're something else."

* * *

My father and stepmother were coming back home the day after my date with Heather. Curious who this mystery woman was, they invited Heather over to have lunch with us. After meeting her, my father pulled me aside and said, "I like her a lot. She's clever, funny, and bright, not like some of those boring girls you've dated."

"Dad, come on."

"I mean it, Alex. Don't let her go. You'll never be lonely or bored in your life with her."

I looked toward Heather then, on the back porch where she was talking with Elisabeth. I'd only spent a handful of hours with her over the past couple of days, but it felt like we were an arrow shot from a bow. My father loved her, Elisabeth loved her, and I could see myself loving her.

And that scared the shit out of me.

It wasn't more than three weeks later when I decided I had to call it off. She was so sure of us, so certain, and it wasn't fair to her that I wasn't. It wasn't fair to her the way I was feeling and how I'd kept it to myself. Rachel had put me through that, and I wasn't about to put someone else through that. I knew things had to end.

I invited her to meet me at a burger place near her apartment in Orlando. With what I was planning to say, I decided the least I could do was drive to her.

We ordered food at the counter and then sat down at a fifties-diner-style booth. A large sheet of paper covered the table, and Heather took a pencil out of her purse and started drawing. By the time our food arrived, she had finished doodling an abstract picture of the top half of an elaborate dragon.

We took bites from our burgers—mine a veggie burger, hers a regular one. I'd practiced my spiel over and over again, but I couldn't think of a word of it as I sat there looking at her. She was beautiful, she expressed her affection for me in a way Rachel never could, and she made me feel at home. But all I wanted was to get in my car and drive away.

Mark had said the insanity of both partners would return time and time again. If I was feeling this insane now, I probably always would. I took a deep breath and cleared my throat.

"Heather, I've had so much fun with you these past few weeks."

Heather immediately stopped chewing and looked up at me through skeptical eyes, but I kept going.

"You're gorgeous, intelligent, and probably one of the funniest people I've ever met. But I don't think this is gonna work."

She quirked an eyebrow. "And why not?"

"My uncle told me that the insanity—"

"Oh, your uncle again." Her laugh had a bite to it.

"No, that's not what I wanted to say. It's just . . . a feeling. This is getting so serious so fast, and I'm sorry, but I'm not ready for it. My last relationship wasn't the best . . . and I'm not really ready for anything too serious right now. I just don't want to lead you on."

She set her burger down and interlaced her fingers on the table. Once again, under a woman's gaze, I felt like a puppy dog with its tail between its legs.

"So you're pushing me away. Why? I'm not Rachel, and I'm not your mom. I'm not going to go cold or walk out or forget you."

"I know that. But—"

"I'm steady," she interrupted. "I'm here. I want to be here for you, but you have to let me. Why won't you let me?"

"I don't know. It's just too much right now."

My knee was bouncing under the table like crazy, and I tried to still it. I *didn't* know. I didn't know if she was actually right for me, and I was just messing it up. I didn't know if my hesitation was a sign we shouldn't be together. I didn't know if it was better to hurt her now, or for her to hurt me now, than sometime later. But in the face of her certainty, I knew my doubt spoke volumes.

She grabbed my hands across the table. Hers were warm and firm. "I don't want to let you go, Alex. We have a really good thing going. Or we did before, you know, this whole conversation."

I shrugged. "It's been three weeks. How could you possibly know that?"

"I knew when I saw your photo. And when we talked on the phone. I told you. It was immediate for me."

I searched her face for the tell: a deadness in the eyes maybe, or a twitch at the corner of her lip. But I couldn't find one. I couldn't come to any conclusion other than that she meant it. Only then did it occur to me that I might be in the pain amplifier yet again, but I wasn't human enough to be able to tell.

I paid attention to my breathing to try to center myself. *"The insanity will return,"* Mark had said, *"unless both parties are willing to work on themselves."* He'd said it was a rare exception.

Heather was ready to be that rare exception for me. But I wasn't ready to be it for her. And that was it.

"I can't give you what you need," I said. "I can't give you the certainty you deserve."

"What are you afraid of?" she asked.

"You think I'm afraid?"

"I know you are." Her tone was firm, concerned.

"Well, I'm not. I just don't want this right now, okay? Don't tell me how I feel when you don't actually know."

She nodded stiffly and pulled her hands away from mine. "For the record, I think you're afraid of abandonment. You know I'm not going anywhere, so you're beating me to the punch. You think you're protecting yourself, but you're the only one you need protection from."

"Now you definitely sound like my uncle."

"Must be a smart guy," she said.

I sulked into my burger. Heather probably thought I sounded as distant and uncertain as Rachel had to me. But Heather and I had only been dating for a few weeks, not three years. That had to make a difference, right? How could anyone be *this* certain after only that long?

We ate the rest of our meal in silence. Heather was quiet on the car ride home, and she didn't call after I got home like she usually did. I thought about calling her instead but didn't.

* * *

On a sunny afternoon a few days later, Mark and I were watching a UF vs. Arkansas game on the couch in his garage. The garage door was open, letting in a warm breeze. I'd taken wheatgrass, completed my meditation, and gone for a walk, but clarity on the situation with Heather was hard to come by.

Mark was disassembling an old cigar lighter and mumbling to himself.

"They don't make them like this anymore," he said, holding up a mechanism from the lighter.

"Why don't you just buy a new one? You can afford it. You're a doctor," I said.

"And you're a shmuck," he said. "You're going to tell me how I should spend my money? Who are you to judge?"

"I guess I didn't think it was a big deal."

"Hologram, remember?"

I didn't push it because I knew he was right. The world is like a hologram, he'd say—the small reflects the whole. On the micro scale, telling someone how to spend their money seemed like a small affront. But on the whole, I was attempting to manipulate him into doing what I thought was best, in a way that was inappropriate. There was no argument I could make against that.

"And while we're at it . . ." He set the lighter parts on the coffee table and turned to me. "Do you happen to know where the herbs for the protein shakes went?"

"Oh, I used the last of them."

"And then you didn't replace them?"

"I guess not. I'm sorry."

"You're not to use them for another month. You need to learn to respect others' things. Actually, you must treat others' things with even greater care than your own. My teacher wouldn't be as forgiving as I am."

"Okay, it won't happen again."

On the screen, the UF coach was screaming soundlessly at the referee. His face was red and bulging.

"Mark, what was your teacher like?" I asked.

He tilted his head toward the right and looked off into space. "Ed was a tough nut, but only because he had to be." He paused for a moment. "I wanted to become a master, Alex. The obstacle is that you can't be told the information—you have to recognize it yourself. And I was deep in my illusions. I could find excuses for everything. Once, he made me stay by myself for three days until I finally faced what I was doing. And from then on, I could see the dramas for what they were."

"What were your dramas?" I asked.

"My first marriage was bad. My wife was absolutely brilliant, but I didn't feel warmth. If I wanted to play the piano, she'd say, 'Lower it down.' Any time I'd try to feel good about myself, she'd say I was bragging. We fought constantly. And I never thought I was worthwhile enough to expect anything better, and so I accepted having a miserable time."

"Why didn't you tell me?" I asked. I remembered walking into his garage in the middle of my drama with Rachel. I remember that look in his eyes like he'd run a marathon in my shoes.

"I'm telling you now because you need to hear it."

Heather floated through my mind. Did he somehow know? Could he sense it on me?

I asked him to tell me the rest of the story, and he did.

* * *

I started the Process when my children were four and six years old. I loved them so much, but I was finding it difficult to go home to my wife at the time. It was too painful to be around her, and the fighting was hurting our children. A friend of mine who was being trained in the Process told me that it didn't have to be this way. I could change my reality. I didn't believe him, but I figured, what did I have to lose? I could learn it like another language. And as I learned more, things started to change.

I began to recognize how much of what I was doing was creating problems. I began to change, and as a result, our marriage improved. My wife even did the Process with me, and we began to relate to each other in a much healthier way.

Then one day, she said she didn't want to do the Process anymore. Mostly because she didn't like Ed, the teacher. Anyway, my wife wanted to go back to marriage counseling instead, which we'd done for eight years with no success. It didn't get any better the second time around. When I was invited to train with the Process in Rio, I asked her to come along. I told her she didn't have to do any of the workshops—it could be just like a second honeymoon and give us a chance to bond again. But she wouldn't come.

I knew then that there was no chance of restoring my

marriage. It felt like dying. I didn't know what would happen to our children, and I was afraid. Something in me told me to go to Rio anyway. I needed to save myself, save my mind, and save our children.

Three months later I was in Rio. On New Year's Eve, in Brazil, they have this tradition where the people make an offering to the goddess of the sea, Yemanjá, in return for a wish or favor. As I understand, Yemanjá is an archetype equivalent to Netzach in Judaism or the Greek Aphrodite. Just as I am viewed differently by others—father, son, husband, brother, teacher, doctor, etc.—depending on the observer, and just as white light is made up of all the colors of the rainbow, so Yemanjá is a "face" or an aspect of the supernal force or being.

At some point after midnight, a group of about fifteen of us dressed in white headed to the seashore. They said I would see the waves grow when the beautiful goddess wanted gifts, and I saw it happen. We opened a bottle of Champagne and offered it to the waves. She likes Champagne. The waves grew stronger.

We took a little boat filled with presents that we had each put in, and each of us made our wish. Mine was already ringing in my head: "Please give me my family back. Please change my wife's mind." One last chance.

The waves were strong. We put the boat at the shoreline, and the waves grabbed the boat and pulled it into the ocean. One wave came back, dumping only my present. Then the ocean went flat and calm.

Yemanjá had given me a quick and certain no. My marriage was over. Not even a powerful goddess could help me.

That evening, we all went to this popular disco club in Ipanema to have dinner. Almost everyone was coupled up except for me. I was feeling really depressed about my marriage and my family, so I thought I'd cheer myself up by trying to dance with someone. I only knew three words in Portuguese, but I thought, what the heck?

I gathered up my courage and motioned to a girl to dance. She danced with me for five minutes but didn't look at me once. Now I was really down.

I was about to leave and go back to my room when I saw these two women and a guy at the front of the dance floor. I tapped one of the women on the shoulder and wiggled my hands in the air. She looked at me and smiled real big, and her eyes were shining. (Little did I know that she'd just had a fever.)

We began dancing, and as she started talking, I responded with the three words of Portuguese I actually knew: I don't speak Portuguese. She laughed. She really didn't want an American. She was looking for somebody local. Nevertheless, she gave me a chance and eventually her phone number. To make a long story short, I kept coming back to Brazil to romance her, and Eunice and I fell in love and eventually got married.

Now, to see the magic, you need to look at the big picture. I'm a doctor; she's a nurse who has since worked with me as a team for decades. Coincidence? Maybe. I asked for family: Nice (her nickname) is number eleven of twelve siblings from a small town in southern Brazil. In her family, each person helped one another until all finished college and had successful careers. All our families, including myself, remain very close.

When seven months later, after my divorce was final, I brought Nice to meet my children, it took my daughter less than five minutes to bond with her. It took my four-year-old son a day and a half. They've loved her, I mean really loved her, ever since. My daughter even took Portuguese in college so she could talk with my wife in her native language, even though Nice speaks excellent English. When Nice became pregnant, both kids were excited to have a new brother, never having any jealousy. To this day they are extremely close.

I asked Yemanjá for my family, and she said, "I can't give you the wish as you ask for it, but I am going to give you one of my own."

My first marriage had ended, which tore me apart, but I was given something even greater. If Ed hadn't helped me to see myself, dissolve my illusions, and teach me the Process, I might never have left my first wife, I might never have met Eunice, and I might never have become your teacher.

* * *

Once Mark had finished telling the story, he turned to me. "So, Alex. Do you understand?" he asked.

"I do. It's an incredible story. You and Nice are so great together. It's like fate."

Mark shook his head. "The gift, Alex. Pay attention to the gifts that get sent back. What you wished for might be elsewhere."

Just then, it clicked. I realized that the waves *had* sent back my gift. I'd asked the universe for happiness, for companionship, for fun. I'd assumed this would mean spending a few years dating before settling down with somebody. But the universe had something else in mind. And like Mark's choice to approach Nice on the dance floor, I had to be the one to claim the gift that was already in front of me. The person whom I'd let fear turn me away from.

"How did you know?" I asked Mark.

He shrugged, smiling warmly. "Don't you have somewhere to be?"

I thanked Mark, jumped in my car, and drove straight to Heather's house in Orlando. The sky was as blue and open as the sea. I hardly noticed the time passing as I drove. When she answered the door, she was wearing pale-blue sweatpants and a white tank top.

"Why are you here?" she asked flatly.

"You're right," I started. "I am afraid. I'm afraid of being the person I was in my last relationship. I'm afraid of falling flat on my face again. But I think more than anything, I'm afraid of you."

She crossed her arms. "Afraid of me? Why?"

"I am!" I exhaled quickly. "I'm afraid of you. You're so sure of me, but I'm bound to disappoint you. Like, inevitably. And the thought of disappointing you or hurting you or just getting hurt again terrifies me."

"So noble," she teased.

"It does. The way you look at me scares me. The future you talk about scares me. It all freaking scares me, Heather."

She took a barefooted step toward me. "And yet, here you are."

"And yet, here I am."

We stood there looking at each other for a while before I brought my hand up to her cheek, running my thumb along her jawline. Incredibly, my mind was almost blank, and when I spoke, it seemed to come through me rather than out of me.

"I think we're the rare exception," I said.

"What?" she asked, laughing.

"Someone told me that a relationship won't work unless both people are willing to put the effort in. To grow together. To work through the flaws and the fears. Well, I think we could be that rare exception."

"Only one way to find out," she said.

CHAPTER 6

* * *

Light and Dark

Fear is the path to the dark side. Fear leads to anger. Anger leads to hate. Hate leads to suffering.

—Yoda, *Star Wars: Episode I—The Phantom Menace* (1999 film)

On a warm morning in March, Heather and I were lying together on the couch at my dad's house, our legs intertwined. She was watching *Friends* on TV while I dragged my finger across the page of a thick LSAT study guide. As usual, my mind wasn't cooperating. Every word I read felt as indecipherable as a baby's babbling. When my eyes lingered on the TV screen for too long, Heather smacked my leg and pointed to the book.

"Focus, Alex! Do I need to turn this off?"

"No. I just don't think I'm cut out for this." I shut the book and threw it on the coffee table, then wiped my eyes with the backs of my hands. "I don't even know if I want to be a lawyer."

"You *are* cut out for this—you're just psyching yourself out again."

"I don't know. I can't focus at all. Maybe I just don't care enough."

"Here, wait a minute."

Heather gently untangled her legs from mine and walked into our home office, then returned with a framed plaque. Inside the plaque was a white piece of paper with words typed in a small font on it. She crossed her legs under the coffee table and passed the plaque to me.

"Read it out loud and stop being a silly goose."

The certificate read:

This letter is regarding your application to the Heather School of Law. We were thoroughly impressed with your application, and we have the distinct pleasure of informing you of your acceptance to our program. In addition to our law classes, the Heather School of Law teaches respect, certainty, spirituality, and health. We expect you will be our top student, and your work will be greatly appreciated.

I felt my smile extend from ear to ear. "You're the best, Heather. This is super thoughtful."

"Hang it up in your bathroom or somewhere you can look at it every day. The way I see it, you're already a law student. You've done all the work, studied, prepared for the test, and now they just have to make it official by giving you the title. You've got this in the bag!"

"It's just . . . What if this isn't the right path for me? I didn't really explore my options in college. I love animals—maybe I'm supposed to be a vet. And psychology. I always loved psychology. And with my training in the Process, wouldn't I be good at counseling?"

With that thought, for the first time in weeks, I felt a weight being lifted from my shoulders, my chest expanding. *That's it*, I thought. *That's what I'm here to do.*

"Be back soon!" I said, then kissed Heather on the cheek and left the plaque on the coffee table.

"Wait, where are you—Alex!"

But I was already headed out the door on my way to Mark's house.

* * *

I found Mark playing the piano, an upbeat rock song I hadn't heard before.

"Mark!" I exclaimed. "I've figured it out. I want to be a psychologist."

He stopped playing and looked at me quizzically. "Oh? What about law school?"

"Well, I loved studying psychology in college. With what you've taught me, I could help so many more people in talk therapy, or in addiction counseling or something."

"Bullshit. Why are you performing another drama for me?"

"What? This isn't a drama. I just don't think law is my calling."

"So instead, you want to work with people who may not want to get better? You're going to have the patience to listen to people's problems, provide some advice, and then watch as the majority don't change?"

I frowned. "I didn't think of it that way."

"What you're saying doesn't match up with reality. This is a clear indication you're insane. Did you use the Tools?"

"No."

"Go—"

"Meditate," I interrupted, my shoulders drooping. "Fine, I will."

I went into the spare room and began to meditate. As the adrenaline in my body slowly dissipated, the truth became clear. I nearly laughed out loud at how quickly I could lose my grip on reality.

When an hour had passed, I met Mark back at the piano bench. Now he was playing "Greenfields" by the Brothers Four. Mark's gray head bobbed along to the melody, and his hands moved as deftly as someone in their twenties.

He stopped playing and turned to me. "So, my little Freud, what's the verdict?"

"I don't want to be a psychologist. I'm just scared."

"And what are you afraid of?"

Always that question—and always an answer to it. "The LSAT. What if I fail? What if I don't get into a good law school?"

Mark smiled. "I didn't go to an Ivy League medical school. But what initials do I have at the end of my name?"

"MD."

"That's right. You're torturing yourself again. You must like pain, huh?"

"I don't!"

"Could have fooled me." He chuckled. "Remember, reality is . . ."

"What is."

Mark nodded. "Have you been studying?"

"I've tried to."

"I'll tell you straight, Alex. If you put in the work, you will get accepted to law school. Period. You know what to do now."

"Face the fear?" I asked, though that was obviously the answer.

"You must always face your fears. Otherwise, they'll keep coming back. There is no escape. You have to move forward with courage."

So, with Heather's and Mark's help, that's exactly what I did. I got back home, grabbed a hammer and nail from the garage, and hung Heather's acceptance plaque next to the bathroom mirror. And for the next two months, I studied for hours almost every day.

When I performed well on the LSAT, I was happy enough, but I knew the hardest hurdle lay ahead. After a few months of sending out applications, and an agonizing wait for decisions, in February I received a letter from my preferred school. I called Heather into our living room and, together, we opened the letter slowly and cautiously. Incredibly,

I'd been accepted. We rejoiced and hugged and laughed. For a whole hour, I replayed Willy Wonka's "(I've Got a) Golden Ticket" and sang along until my throat hurt.

I called Mark to tell him the news.

"Mark, I got into law school!"

"I'm not surprised, Alex."

"I can't believe this," I said. "I'm over the moon. I did it!"

"Yes, you did, but be careful. Never get too high or too low."

"But isn't this worthy of celebrating?"

"Celebrate, absolutely. But staying too high or too low creates adrenaline, moving you toward insanity. Puts you at risk for making poor decisions and creating more suffering for yourself and for others."

"What goes up . . . ?"

"That's right. Take everything with a grain of salt. There's no way for you to know what this path will hold. Like stud poker, you don't control the cards you're given, but you can choose how to play them—how to make the best of them. So, do the best that you can with the cards you are dealt."

* * *

As always, Mark turned out to be right, though not in the way we expected.

During my first year of law school, I filed a lawsuit against my former real estate broker who refused to pay some of the commissions he owed me. I represented myself, *pro se*. (Of course, later in my legal career, I heard the joke that only a foolish lawyer represents himself.)

Despite what I thought was a well-constructed argument, the court did not rule in my favor. I was debating whether or not to appeal and decided to ask Mark the next time I saw him.

"Did you do the work?" he asked while we were sitting in our usual spots in the garage.

"Yes."

He shrugged. "Then appeal."

"I'm afraid I'll just lose again."

"There you go with the fear," Mark said.

"It's a lot of paperwork to file. It could be a big waste of time and effort."

"It's the principle, Alex. Never back down to a bully. By standing up to a bully, whether you win or lose, you demonstrate character. In fact, I'll pay the court fees. If you win, give me back double my investment. If you lose, don't worry about paying me back."

So I went through with the appeal. Unfortunately, I ended up losing the case, but I learned an important lesson. I put in the work. I did what was right without concern for the external outcome. And I focused on the intrinsic reward that was my own self-respect.

* * *

After three years of law school, I'd passed the bar exam, and the only thing standing in the way of being a licensed lawyer was a meeting with the bar examiners.

The morning of the meeting, I showered, shaved my face close, and put on a tailored navy suit and brown loafers. By this time, Heather and I were living together in a small apartment in South Florida. I walked downstairs to find our little dog, Mordi, which Heather had gotten us a couple of years before, greeting me with a whip-fast wagging tail. He was a feisty, white Jack Russell terrier with two big brown spots covering his ears and the fur around his eyes. He also had a little brown splotch on top of his head that looked like a prayer cap, which had inspired his Jewish old-man name, Mordecai—Mordi for short.

He'd been a surprise from Heather ("An impulse buy near the register," as she would say jokingly), but he'd quickly become my best buddy. Mordi would hang out with me whenever I studied, and Heather and I took him everywhere with us, including on road trips. When my camera bag was on the floor, he'd always bite the strap and run around in circles, swinging it over his head like some circus trick before tripping over it. When I needed a walk to re-center, I'd often take him with me, the stocky lower half of his body wiggling from side to side as he trotted along. He loved chasing ducks, and one time he got stuck in a float of debris near the lake's center. I almost drowned going after him, diving into the lake in my jeans to save him. Not my idea of fun, but it was definitely memorable.

On this important morning, Heather had made breakfast, and we sat down together at the small kitchen table to eat.

"How are you?" she asked.

I shrugged. "I have a bad feeling about today."

Heather smiled at me, but her face looked strained. "I'm not worried," she said. "You're going to do great. If you stay calm and speak with intention, you'll pass with flying colors."

But something in her voice sounded insincere—or at least withholding.

"Would you tell me if you had an intuition I was going to fail royally?"

She laughed. "I absolutely would not tell you. But that's not what this is, I promise! You got this."

Heather and I cleaned up the dishes, then drove to the bar examiner center in Orlando. Before I ventured in, I took a deep breath with both hands on the wheel, then walked toward the large conference center at the Orlando International Airport. I looked back at Heather as I walked, and she gave me a thumbs-up from the car.

I found the conference room that they'd indicated in their email on the second floor. Inside the big, bare room, three examiners sat on one side of a long wooden table, two men and a woman. I shook each of their hands and took a seat in the metal foldout chair across from them.

They riffled through my paperwork and asked me standard questions about my academic history, my experience, and my motivations for earning this degree. All of this

I'd prepared for. But then they brought up something that floored me.

The female examiner adjusted her glasses, clasped her hands on the table, and said, "Mr. Nottingham, your former real estate broker submitted an allegation of fraud to us. What do you say to this?"

My stomach sank. I thought I'd done what was right. I'd stood up to a bully—and because of that, I might be denied access to the bar. And besides that, all my training in the Process, just to be called a fraud? It felt terrible having my name even spoken alongside that word.

"I didn't commit fraud," I responded, and then explained the situation to them as I'd presented it in court before.

One of the male examiners shook his head. He had a thick black mustache and dark, kind eyes. "We'll have to take some time to learn more about the situation and make our decision then. We'll send you in writing our determination for your bar admittance."

After I pushed the door open and started walking down the tiled hallway, I called Mark and told him what had happened.

"Well, did you commit fraud?" he asked.

"Of course not!"

"So what's there to be concerned about?"

"That they won't accept me. That I'll have to do more appeals. I mean, fraud! I hate this guy."

"Yeah, that's what bullies do. But why lose your cool?"

Standing in front of the elevator, I smashed the down

button and waited for it to arrive. "Because I've worked so hard for this, and now it could be taken away from me. All because of a lie!"

"Trust in the power of certainty," Mark said seriously.

I rubbed my temples with my fingers. Finally, the elevator dinged, and the doors opened with a whoosh. I stepped inside. "What do you mean?"

"The Process teaches us that when you act in good faith and put in the work, things always work out. Always. You can trust certainty. I have no doubt, zero, that you'll get accepted to the bar."

"I don't know about that."

"Alex," he said, "what's the point of worrying?"

"I can't help it," I said.

"Nonsense! I can teach you how to never worry again. First, remember these two laws of the universe: Number one, you have to put in the work. And second, you can only do what you can do. Alex, can you do more than what you can do?"

I laughed. "I guess not."

"Okay. So no matter what you're worrying about, you have three options. First, you can do nothing. If a car is coming at you and you don't get out of the way, you're going to get hit. So that doesn't work."

"Right," I said. The elevator doors opened and I was deposited on the first floor of the building. I walked outside into the late May heat, phone to my ear and listening intently.

"The second option is you put in the work, but you worry

what's going to happen. Does the worry help anything? No. Does the worry give you any advantages? No. It makes you feel bad. It makes the people who care about you feel bad. Is there anything right about asking for pain with no benefit?"

"Of course not," I said.

"Exactly!" I could picture Mark's wide eyes on the other side of the phone. "But you have a third choice. You can say, 'I'm gonna do what I can do.' As long as it's the *best* you can do. You put a smile on your face and say, '*Que sera, sera*. I'm not gonna worry about that outcome. I'm going to appreciate what I have.' You can see, you can hear, you got your arms, you got your legs, you got food in your belly, a roof over your head, you're living here in paradise."

I waved at Heather in the car and motioned that I'd be right over. "I know, Mark. It's just that this guy might cost me my entire career—"

"There it is!" Mark boomed. "When you start worrying, pay attention. Slow down, realize you're worrying, and if you put in the work, forget about the outcome. Soon you'll find out that the things you worry about don't come true. Whatever happens, let it be."

I nodded. "Okay, I think I can do that. Thanks, Mark."

Two months passed, and I received a letter from the Florida bar. Nervously, I opened the letter: "We've reviewed the broker's claims against you and found no merit in them. Alexander Nottingham, we're pleased to admit you to the Florida bar."

I nearly jumped out of my seat! And all I could think about was how useless it had been to ever worry.

* * *

Shortly before we got engaged to be married, Heather began training in the Process with me. She'd seen how much the Tools and teachings had helped me navigate my life and wanted to know if they could help her too. We'd meditate together, Mordi stretched out between us, snoring.

But in the early days of our engagement, Heather and I would get into these epic battles at home—and especially on road trips—over the seemingly smallest things, so we decided to go to Mark's to talk with him about it. He instructed us to watch the movie *Krull* beforehand.

We sat around Mark's dining table, eating egg salad sandwiches and potato chips.

"Remember what I taught you, that the universe presents itself in threes?" Mark asked.

Heather and I both nodded. I thought back to my first training session with Mark: protons, neutrons, electrons; id, ego, and superego.

"And do you remember the three parts of each of your psyches?"

We both thought for a moment, recalling the teaching but not the details. Heather said, "The Inner, Middle, and Higher Selves?"

Mark clapped his hands together. "Exactly. First, let's make sure we have our definitions straight. Your Inner Self is memory and emotion, your source of energy, your zest for life. Your Middle Self is your reason, the logical part. It protects and guides you, and it keeps you safe from danger. It provides you with systems and overlays to function in the world. And your Higher Self transcends all parts. It's your direct connection to Source, the universe, God—whatever that means to you. Your Higher Self is your inspiration, love, creativity, and freedom."

As Mark was talking, I took a couple of chips from Heather's plate and ate them since I'd already finished mine.

She shot me a look. "What the hell?"

"What?" I asked. "I'm still hungry."

"You know I hate when you take food off my plate!"

"It's just chips! I'm sure there's more in the kitchen."

"It's not about that, Alex!"

Mark smiled like an amused sage. "All right, kids. Settle down, settle down."

"Mark, tell him how disrespectful that is," Heather said. "He always does this. How hard is it to ask first?"

I balked. "Mark was talking! I didn't want to interrupt."

"Ahh, synchronicity is at work again." Mark winked. "May I continue?"

We both nodded, shrinking like kids in the principal's office.

"Both the Middle and Inner Self can derail. However, the Inner Self is what creates a lot of day-to-day dysfunctions. And because of its emotional programs, it can lead to insanity."

Heather asked, "And I guess that's what's happening with us right now?"

"Clearly," Mark said good-naturedly.

"So what do we do when we get derailed or lose sanity?" I asked.

Mark sang the next line like it was a jingle: "*Use the four-letter word!*"

"Oh, we use a *lot* of those," Heather joked.

"No, no." Mark laughed. "Use the word 'stop.' S-T-O-P. Think of how in a movie, the action will stop, but you can still hear the main character's thoughts. It's just like that. You have to stop the world for a moment, so you can ask: What am I doing? What *should* I be doing? This moves you from a *reactive* personality to a thinking personality. It allows you to break free from your reactive Inner Self and tune in to your *proactive* Middle Self."

"Got it," I said. "So we should say 'stop' and then use the Tools?"

"That's correct. After you meditate, you'll become sane, naturally lowering your reactivity and connecting you with your Middle Self."

"What's so bad about the Inner Self?" Heather asked. "Sometimes it's good to get angry, to let it out. Are you saying I should keep everything bottled up?"

"Not at all. Your Inner Self is not inherently bad, it just needs to be guided and protected by your Middle Self. The

Inner Self is like a child. Do you want a child to make decisions in your life?"

"Nope," we said in unison.

"That's right. Kids are adorable bundles of fun. But what happens when they lose control, either from fear or anger? They're totally reactive—insane. That's what's happening with not only you but all human beings. You think you're talking to adults all day. But typically, you're dealing with a bunch of inner selves."

"That all makes sense," Heather said. "But what am I *supposed* to do when Alex pisses me off?"

I smirked. "Well, you *have* mastered the art of the passive-aggressive eye roll."

"Don't use sarcasm," Mark said. "Do you know what sarcasm literally means? To tear at the flesh."

"But I was just joking," I said.

"There is no such thing as joking. There are opportunities to be funny, for sure. The issue is when it is at someone else's expense. If you use what I teach you and are mindful of what is really going on, you'll realize you're attacking their Inner Self."

"I never looked at it that way."

"See if you can notice the sick, dark pleasure you get from hurting someone. Sarcasm and 'just joking' are examples of passive aggressiveness, just like you accused Heather of."

"Well, now I feel bad."

"You should!" Heather said.

"You're both looney tunes. Remember the story of

Humpty Dumpty? Your words are like that. You may say something in anger that you can't take back, and Humpty Dumpty—things can't be put back together again. Be careful about what you say to each other. Not everything can be repaired. Go meditate on all of this."

Together we went into the spare bedroom, crossed our legs on the floor, and leaned against the bed. I closed my eyes, listening to the cars pass by and the muffled sound of the TV show Mark had turned on in the living room. I heard Heather's quiet breathing beside me. My breaths were shallow, but I tried to avoid fighting the discomfort.

After about thirty minutes, Mark opened the door.

"So, who were you being before?"

"Our inner selves," Heather said. "Whiny babies."

Mark raised up his hands. "You said it, not me! So now that you're sane, tell me what was really going on."

I replied first, saying, "I wasn't being sensitive to Heather's needs. I should ask before eating her food."

"And I shouldn't have yelled at him," Heather said. "I could've expressed myself more kindly."

"Look at all this beautiful sanity!" Mark smiled. "Remember, you two are mirrors for each other. What you don't like in your partner is what you don't like in yourself."

"What do you mean?" I asked. "I don't get mad if she eats my food."

"You're missing the point." Mark walked to the foot of the bed and sat down. He pointed at me.

"Alex, you created a situation for Heather to attack

you, so in reality, you attacked her." He turned to Heather. "Heather, your reaction to Alex created a situation where you were disrespectful. You both created this, and you both suffered for it."

"Okay," I said. "But I still don't get how attacking her is the same thing as attacking myself."

He continued, "Both of you have a cross-sex self. Alex, you have a female self within you, and Heather, you have a male self within you. Think of the yin-yang symbol: the dot of white in the center of the black."

It took a moment to recall the symbol Mark was referencing, but we both nodded in recognition.

Mark continued: "Alex, when you disrespect Heather, you are actually damaging your cross-sex self—the female within you. Heather, it's the same with your inner male self. In a relationship, you want both polarities—male and female energies—to be cared for and honored. When working properly, these energies make you stronger. But much of the time, the couple is unaware of just how much their dramas are directed at themselves rather than the other person."

"So we say STOP, use the Tools, and recognize how much we've contributed to the situation," I said. "I think we can do that."

"That's a great start. A healthy marriage spells a healthy life. Did you get a chance to watch *Krull*?" Mark asked.

"We did," I replied.

"And?"

"It wasn't as good as *Dune*."

"The point of the movie is how darkness follows the light," Mark noted.

"Right," Heather said. "Like how that castle with the beast came to interrupt the marriage between the main characters."

"Yes. Whenever there is goodness or Light, then evil or Dark will come. The teaching is to be mindful of this. When life is going well, be prepared. Darkness will find a way to sabotage. When one partner attacks the other partner, they're feeding the dark side. And it feels kinda good, right?"

"In the moment, yeah," Heather said. "Like I'm getting something off my chest."

"Well, expect a short circuit real soon," Mark said. "You're gonna feel great with darkness. You're gonna feel high. But then you're going to feel a low. You're causing pain that you'll feel later. That's how it works—anger, which is a form of fear, is fueled by darkness. You feel a twisted self-righteous good, but then you experience pain. With the Process, you learn to disrupt the cycle. You see the pattern and break it before it continues. You go, 'Ah, I know who you are. I'm choosing the light instead.'"

Mark continued, "In the movie *Krull*, there was the sacred marriage. Their love was able to defeat the beast only by them standing together. The beast was the dark wanting to separate the couple. This is the only way it can defeat the light. What do you think is happening in your relationship?"

"We fight because the dark side is trying to divide us?" I said, wondering out loud.

"Bingo!" Mark exclaimed. "Both of you took the bait. And not just that, you got self-righteous and fed off the darkness. Don't do it. Remember your partner reflects a part of you. When you beat up your partner, you beat up a part of yourself. The only exception to this is if you're in a truly abusive or bad relationship—then the only choice is to leave."

"You're right," I said.

"Let's look at the consequences too. Alex, do you think the grass is greener? Do you know anyone besides Heather who will put up with your dramas?"

"No," I said.

"Heather, are you going to find a man that works on himself and appreciates you like Alex?"

"No," Heather said.

"Exactly. So stop being looney tunes and make it work!" Mark said, then laughed loudly.

* * *

In November of 2009, Heather and I got married. Our wedding featured the beautiful songs of the cantor, the smashed glass, the chuppah, and our friends lifting us up in our chairs. I felt we had decades of growth and happiness to look forward to.

Mark had a chance to speak at the reception. He had written his speech on an unlined sheet of white paper shortly after the ceremony—he'd recorded whatever came up for him in the moment, he told me later. He wore a three-piece black suit and kept his eyebrows raised as he read from the sheet as if to emphasize every word.

"There will always be disagreements," he'd said. "But if you want your marriage to last, it is better to be warm and magnanimous than right. I know you're both very smart, but where your partner's concerned, choose the warmth of the heart."

His words would prove invaluable in our marriage. But just a couple of years later, this advice would help me navigate another situation—with my mother.

* * *

In 2011, my mother left her second husband. She'd just gotten back from a cruise with him when he admitted he'd been cheating on her. Once she set foot in Miami, she basically drove straight to South Florida to stay at Heather's and my apartment. That was a long couple of days. Heather and I argued fiercely while she was there; the whole energy of the place felt out of balance and chaotic. One day, when my mom was on one of her manic dramas, she went into our bathroom and, without asking anyone, threw out half of Heather's belongings—makeup, beauty supplies, hair products—saying they were all crappy or expired. That was the last proverbial straw. We helped my mother find a condo, and she moved in as soon as the purchase was finalized. It was only two blocks away from my father and stepmother's house, a bold move even for her.

I visited her a week after she moved in, and she'd already put the condo together. The movers had come and gone, and the boxes had all been emptied. Most of the furniture was tan, white, and neutral, except for one painting of a bundle of red hibiscus flowers that hung on the living room wall. There was a large cat tree to the right of the TV stand where her cat—a gray one with white socks named Jasper—stared at me anxiously. He scurried into her bedroom soon after he saw me.

She didn't stand up when I came in, so I sat beside her on the couch and gave her a hug. She kept her arms at her sides, her silk shirt crumpling. Her hazel-brown eyes looked far away, and a halo of very curly blondish-brown hair framed her face.

"James is a good-for-nothing," she said. "People tried to warn me. Our neighbor Marsha wouldn't stop going on about it. But I didn't believe her." She laughed coldly.

"I'm sorry about all this," I said half-heartedly. She'd told the story at least a dozen times while she was staying with us, and here it was again. But it was useless to interrupt her. She would keep going regardless.

"Me too—but not really. We hadn't been solid for years. He probably would've walked out if I didn't. He had plenty of second-stringers ready to go, turns out." She noticeably softened her gaze. "Listen, Alexander, I need your help."

I'd known this was coming. I guessed she wanted to have a semblance of independence before asking the big question.

"You know I don't have anything except what's in this

shoebox of a place. I've worked out what I need to get by, and it's not much. And you're all I've got to rely on."

I eyed the two orange pill bottles on the coffee table. Only two. Maybe they were nothing to worry about—just her prescriptions. I tried to remember if she was on antidepressants, Xanax, or something else, but I thought it best not to ask.

"I'll have to think about it," I told her.

She grabbed my hand in hers. "It wouldn't be all that much. Please, Alexander. My friend Annie's son takes care of her."

"Yeah, because he was raised by his mom."

"Oh, please. Like you had it so rough."

That stung. She hadn't been there for me when I needed her, so what did I owe her now? But I allowed myself to sit with the old pain this was bringing up. I breathed. I remembered that I would be helping to create a bad situation if I reacted blindly to my emotions. Once I'd collected myself, I moved her hand back to her lap and gave it an awkward pat.

"I promise I'll think about it." That was all I could say.

That evening, I went to Mark and Nice's house with Heather, my dad, and my stepmother to have dinner. When I started telling him the situation, Mark urged me to use the Tools first: a shot of wheatgrass and then a meditation. Afterward, I asked my family for their advice.

My father and Elisabeth both encouraged me to help her. Heather assured me she'd support whatever decision I made. With tenderness, Nice looked me directly in the eyes and lovingly said, "She is your mother. If you can help your mother, help her."

I knew that in one way, Nice was right. I existed because of this woman, and didn't that count for something? But part of me felt it wasn't that simple.

"I'm worried she'll just keep using drugs, and I'll be the one supporting it," I said. "What if I'm the reason she hurts herself—or worse?"

Mark said, "In this situation, there's only so much you can do. Have I told you the Taoist story of the farmer?"

He hadn't, so he went on:

A farmer and his son had a beloved horse who helped the family earn a living. One day, the horse ran away, and their neighbors exclaimed, "What terrible luck!" The farmer replied, "Maybe so, maybe not."

A few days later, the horse returned home, leading a few wild horses back to the farm as well. The neighbors shouted out, "What great luck!" The farmer replied, "Maybe so, maybe not."

Later that week, one of the new horses threw the farmer's son to the ground, breaking his leg. The neighbors cried, "What terrible luck!" The farmer replied, "Maybe so, maybe not."

A few weeks later, soldiers marched through town, recruiting boys for the national army. They passed over the farmer's son because of his broken leg. The neighbors shouted, "What tremendous luck!" To which the farmer replied, "Maybe so, maybe not."

"In other words," Mark said, "there's no way for you to know what this path will hold. *Que sera, sera*—whatever will be, will be. Do the best you can do and let go of the rest."

What was the best I could do? I thought about it for a long time, for the rest of dinner and on the ride home, and once I was lying in bed, my eyes trained on the ceiling. My mother had been absent for most of my life, and I knew that part of me still hadn't forgiven her for that. I didn't even know how to forgive her, really, and I was sure that, eventually, I'd have to wade through those waters. But what was most important was that I controlled how I would react. I could choose not to play out my "poor me" drama about her absence, which would lead me to avoid helping her out of spite. And I could accept that even if I did help her, it might not end the way I wanted it to. I only had control of my own actions, not the outcome.

Mark had taught me that independence was the most important thing you could give to someone. But I couldn't use my stinginess to try to force my mother's independence. I couldn't take away her agency like that.

It was 1 AM when I finally decided to call her. I pulled the covers back, and in a matter of moments, Mordi's furry white-and-brown snout poked out from under the covers curiously. He liked sleeping under the blanket, staying warm by my feet. I scratched his head and told him I'd be right back.

I knew Mom would be up watching her crime documentaries like she usually was. She answered after a couple of rings.

"Hello?

"Hey, Mom. I've decided to help you," I said. I was

standing in the living room, talking softly into my cell phone, so I wouldn't wake Heather or rouse Mordi again.

"Oh, Alexander, thank you. Thank you so much."

"But I have a condition."

She was silent for a beat. "What condition?"

I took a deep breath. "I want you to stop using. I know you had a hard childhood, Mom. I know you numb yourself to forget. But I can't be the reason you continue to hurt yourself."

More silence. "You talk like I have control over it."

"You do. We all do. We all create our own worlds with our decisions . . ."

"Don't use that airy-fairy stuff with me. I didn't get a say in what happened to me. I didn't get to make a decision when he . . ." She trailed off and then went quiet again. I imagined her eyes going blank and drifting to the tan rug in her living room.

"I know," I said. "But you survived it. You're here, now. And you can choose what the rest of your life is going to look like. I can help you do that. All you have to do is ask."

I clenched my jaw. I thought I'd gotten over this—trying to change her, to help her. I knew you couldn't help someone who didn't want it. And I knew taking this tack with my mother only pushed her farther away.

"I'm tired. I'm going now. But thanks again, really."

"You're welcome, Mom."

The call ended. At that moment, I felt good about the

decision, but I knew only time would tell how it would play out.

* * *

When Heather got pregnant in March of 2013, we were beside ourselves with joy. About four months into pregnancy, we went into Mark's office to get the ultrasound and find out the baby's gender. When the baby finally stopped wiggling long enough for me to see what it was, I started sobbing happy tears.

Nice, who is also Mark's nurse in his practice, saw me crying after coming out of the ultrasound room. She asked, "You're having a boy, huh?"

I asked her how she knew, and she responded, "Men typically cry when they have their boy. I'm so happy for you guys."

During the pregnancy, Heather asked Mark if she could hang out at his house when she went into labor since he was her doctor. I guess she figured she could stay comfortable as long as possible and only go to the hospital at the very last minute. But Mark felt it wasn't a good idea, that he shouldn't be too close to the situation emotionally as it could affect his judgment.

It was a Wednesday. Heather and I were over at Mark's house in the evening meditating. I was in a separate room, so I didn't know right away what was happening, but I heard about it later. Heather said she felt weird and a bit nauseated. While I was meditating in the other room, she went to use the restroom when suddenly her water broke. She came out and said to Mark and Nice, "I know you didn't want me to go into labor in your house, but I guess the baby didn't listen to your rules!"

We had taken the classes to prepare for childbirth, and they'd always said one thing that stood out: When your water breaks, it won't be anything like in the movies. Well, for Heather, apparently it was exactly like in the movies, with a big burst of water all over their floor.

Mark came in to tell me what was happening, but he insisted that I finish my meditation first and then we would go to the hospital to get checked in. I bet not too many people have experienced driving to the hospital with their ob-gyn in the car. Mark even walked us through a special entrance to the hospital like VIPs.

When the staff told us there were no private birthing rooms available, Mark once again worked his magic. Apparently, one of the women in a private room wasn't actually in labor. It had been a false alarm, and she was released. It was like we were being reminded once again how magic is always working around us if we have certainty that things will work out. Once Heather had gotten settled in her room, I drove to our house to get our hospital bags.

That night was rough. Heather was in a lot of pain but finally got an epidural at around 4 AM, and then she started to relax and progress. We were both able to get some sleep.

By the next morning, things were moving along. Mark came into the room at 9 AM to check on Heather and see how many centimeters she was.

He said, "Things are looking good, kiddo. You're doing great and progressing nicely. I'm going to come back at around two thirty to deliver you."

He then left the room. But about five minutes later, he returned and said, "I was thinking about something . . . Would you like to deliver now, or do you want to wait until two thirty?"

"I have a choice? Uh, how is that even possible?" she asked.

He said in a singsong voice, "Delivering babies is one of the magical things I do!"

She looked at me and then said, "Why prolong this thing any longer? I'm exhausted. Let's get it going!"

During the delivery, the baby's blood pressure dropped significantly in what is called *bradycardia*. About twenty doctors and nurses all ran into the room at the same time with multiple monitors and alarms going off. I started backing toward the wall and almost fainted. All eyes were on me while poor Heather was trying to deliver a baby. One of the nurses even asked, "Sir, are you okay? Do you feel like you're going to pass out? I can get you a chair if you need it."

But Mark, once again with no worries and supreme confidence, had our baby out in a few minutes, healthy as he could be.

* * *

Everything seemed to be looking up. Our new business, a consulting business, which was born around the same time as our son, was going well; we had our boy, Zachary; we had a sweet and feisty pup; and our relationship seemed to be stronger than ever. On the outside, everything seemed perfect. But the Process wasn't finished with me yet.

The Tools

Ready to bring the magic to life?

I've put together a special companion page where you can download **the Tools** we explore in this book—plus a few surprises, including:

- Step-by-step instructions
- Guided audio meditation
- Recommended resources

Claim your free access here:
http://alexnottingham.com/tools

Your journey is just beginning.

PART 2

* * *

Going Deeper

CHAPTER 7

* * *

Faking It

Every adversity, every failure, every heartache carries with it the seed of an equal or greater benefit.

—Napoleon Hill, *Think and Grow Rich*

Taking a deep breath, I stepped onto the convention stage in the large hotel ballroom. In the audience, sitting in rows and rows of folding chairs, were dozens of dentists and dental professionals, some in business clothes and others in scrubs or white coats. Most looked at least mildly interested in me as I walked toward the podium, but a few were fixated on the phones in their laps or nodding off after a long day of talks. The fluorescent lights felt hot on my skin, and I sensed the sweat beading at my armpits. I prayed it wouldn't show through my blue button-up shirt, but it wasn't what I was most worried about. I couldn't help but think...

No. I pushed that thought away and remembered why I was here. I wanted to make the world around me better in the best way I knew how.

"Good afternoon, everyone!" I said as brightly as I could, then waited for the chatter to die down before continuing. "I'm Alex Nottingham, founder and CEO of All-Star Dental Academy. You've been to a lot of talks already this weekend, but this one will be different. We won't be talking root canals or braces design, or how to pull teeth without losing friends. And despite the name of this talk, I won't be spewing business buzzwords your way. Instead, I want to talk about *you*."

A few eyebrows quirked, and I saw at least two audience members look up from their phones.

"There's a reason you all got into the work you do," I said. "There's a fire there, a story there. And *that* is what you have to drill into, no pun intended, to improve your business. But before we go further, I want to tell you about the first dental practice I ever worked with. And how our team helped bring it from bankrupt to booming."

I told them the story I'd told countless times by this point, pride swelling in my chest just like it always did. It was the story of my own father's dental business.

Though my father is a phenomenal dentist, his business was doing poorly, and about ten years before this talk, his business was approaching bankruptcy. So he agreed to let me help him. First, I encouraged him to change his perception, how he saw his practice and business. He needed to get back to their vision of pursuing phenomenal dentistry. We got clear on his vision and his story, said it over and over again, and from there, totally changed his business's marketing plan from the inside out.

Though this got him more leads, those leads weren't converting to clients. So we asked Heather, who was still my girlfriend at the time, to move to his office from her position as a sales manager and trainer at Bloomingdale's. She started handling all communications with clients and potential clients for the dental practice, like a patient concierge and scheduler of sorts.

"These changes yielded better results than we could have imagined," I said to the audience. "In less than eighteen months, we helped double his business, taking the practice from $1 million and near bankruptcy to over $2.4 million! I decided this is how I could best put my own training to work. So Heather and I founded a business where we could help dental offices get clear on their values and thrive."

By now, I had every audience member's undivided attention. This is how it always went. Who *didn't* want to see those kinds of results for their own practices? I was glad I could have this sort of impact on people. So if I could just focus on the people I was inspiring and not the thoughts nagging at the back of my head, it would be all right. It had to be.

I continued: "Yes, we fixed their marketing. Yes, we fixed their customer service. All that was necessary. But the *catalyst* for it all was my dad's shift in perception, the strengthening of his belief in his original vision, and the reason he got into dentistry in the first place. By a show of hands, how many of you feel overwhelmed by the day-to-day—the insurance companies, the turnover, the bills, the no-shows? How many of you feel disconnected from your original *why*?"

About three-quarters of the audience raised their hands, and more than a few people looked sheepish.

I nodded my head and paused for a moment to allow the atmosphere to reset, walking slowly across the stage. I couldn't help but smile before I spoke again. "That's what I mean when I say I want to talk about *you*. Your passion, your vision, your desire. Someone once told me that there are five steps you must take in order to create anything in this world. And the first step is to access your *desire* to bring something to life."

I pictured Mark's kind face and large hands shaping out these words. When I wanted to start my business, this business, he taught me the five steps to create a world. Now, I was able to share these steps with others, though in a more down-to-earth format. I felt a pang in my chest, but I dismissed it. I had to keep moving forward.

"The first step is *desire*. Without desire, there's no heart in what you do. And without heart, there's no life in what you do. Take a few moments to remember your desire. Write it down if you want to. Connect to it. What made you choose this career? What did you want to accomplish? This exercise can work for any other sector of your life too. Focus on what resonates."

About half the audience bent their heads and either scribbled on their pamphlets or started tapping on their phones. The rest looked thoughtful.

When Mark had asked me these questions, I knew the answers immediately. I wanted to create a business to provide for my family. I'd gone to law school and then gotten my MBA, using both degrees to gain experience and accomplish my goal of having my own business. When Mark told me this was too nebulous and to be more specific, I said I wanted to do business coaching or consulting. I wanted to help people create abundance in their lives and, in turn, help them improve the lives of others. It's the reason I was standing on this stage today. It was the reason that Heather and I were preparing to buy our very first house. And it was the reason that so many people were flourishing where before their heads had been underwater.

"The second step is the *mechanism*, the training and tools you'll require to accomplish what you want to do. You have the training, so I imagine you're great at what you do. Sure, maybe your businesses could use some work, but you can lean on services like mine for support in running your business. So we'll move on to the next step."

"The third step," I continued, "is *enthusiasm*. This is the creative energy, the fun, behind every endeavor. Without enthusiasm, you're liable to burn out. And judging by all the hands that went up, I would imagine many of you could use more of it. Think this over for a few minutes. What stands in the way of your enthusiasm? What would get you more excited about your work? What do you need help with in order to reconnect with that fire?"

I paused a moment. The same people jotted down notes or tapped, and the others seemed to be concentrating, looking off into the distance or toward the on-stage projector screen.

I continued, "The fourth step is *work*. And after however many decades of school and straight As and full workweeks, most of you don't need help in this department. You know you have to put in the time, make the effort, and go the extra mile to be successful."

I reflected on what Mark had told me: "For you specifically, nephew, you can't let your dramas get in the way of the work." He emphasized that there were no shortcuts to this. If I didn't put in the work, I'd get the *bread of shame*—rewards I didn't properly earn. And those rewards would be easily taken from me.

"So we'll move on," I continued to the audience. "The fifth step is to *receive*, to gratefully accept the rewards of your efforts. This sounds like the easy part, right?" That's what I had said when Mark first introduced these steps to me.

"But it's not. There's an impediment to receiving. You can sabotage yourself here. If you say, *Poor me, I'm not good enough for all this*, then you won't properly enjoy your rewards. And if you don't enjoy your rewards, you'll either lose them, or you'll crave more and more and more, without ever feeling satisfied. You have to remember what you're aiming for and celebrate it when you get there. Be grateful."

I asked the audience, "What have you achieved in your business that you struggled to really receive? What has kept you from properly appreciating those achievements? Would you be happier and more connected to your desire and enthusiasm if you allowed yourself to receive it?"

I noticed a woman in her forties in the front row who seemed to have a lightbulb moment. Her eyes widening, she looked off to the left of the stage, lost in thought. Then her pen raced across the back of the convention pamphlet until I spoke again.

"So continue to stay up to date on your training and work hard. But also remember your desire, remove impediments to your enthusiasm, and be open to receiving the fruits of your labor. If you successfully do these five things, you'll be shocked at what you can pull off. Because, hey, it worked for me."

I said a silent thanks to Mark, closed out my talk, and walked down the stage steps. Immediately, the woman who'd appeared to have an epiphany approached me. She had a small, sweet smile and shoulder-length black hair.

"Wonderful talk," she said, extending her hand. "I'm Dr. Iyer. Pleased to meet you."

I took her hand and shook it warmly. "It was my pleasure. What did you find most helpful?"

"So much," she said, beaming. "I come from a very poor family, and now I have kids of my own. I always thought the main reason I wanted to become a dentist was to provide stability for my family, which I never had. But you've helped me realize that I truly love this work. It's not just a vehicle to support my family; it's what inspires me and gives me a sense of purpose. And now I'm bursting with ideas for how to improve my practice."

"That's amazing," I said.

"I can't believe I didn't realize it before. I just know my employees and patients are going to benefit from my renewed energy, not to mention my family. So thank you, Alex. I feel like you've given me my life back."

She took my hands in hers and shook them again. After exchanging business cards, we said goodbye, and I stood at the front of the ballroom and chatted with another dozen or so dentists before returning to my room.

* * *

The plain hotel room door closed behind me with a click. I loosened my tie with my left hand while I grabbed a beer from the mini fridge with my right. I settled down on the made-up bed without taking off my loafers, popped the top on the Coors Light, and turned on the TV to watch the news. But I couldn't sit still. My leg was going and going, and only one word existed in my mind:

Hypocrite.

I'd just returned from giving a talk to a large group of dentists about how to live a balanced life and not settle for mediocrity, yet here I was, unbalanced, not using the Tools, and not taking care of myself. The irony was obvious. I'd gained thirty pounds in the last year, sweets and salty foods like pizza and chips being my weakness. I traveled all the time for work and hardly saw my wife or three-year-old son. And I wasn't sure how I'd gotten here, so far off track from where I'd been even a couple of years before.

The female newscaster with perfect blond hair and a toothpaste grin talked about the new weight-loss drug, the upcoming Brexit decision, and horrifying shootings. All this chaos and hardship in the world, yet I couldn't control my own mind, not even after years of fixating on it. I finished off my beer and got up to get another one.

I pulled off one shoe at a time and lay back down on the bed, doing what I'd done so many nights before—thinking hard yet getting nowhere. I remembered a conversation I'd had with Mark early on in our lessons when I still wanted to use the Process for my own gain. *Maybe that hasn't changed*, I thought grimly.

"What about the green stuff?" I had asked him while we sat in his garage watching a football game one day in the fall. It felt like a lifetime ago, but I was surprised to realize that only about five years had passed since then.

"Weed?" Mark replied.

I laughed. "No, money."

"Ah. I'm a child of the sixties, so I could tell you stories." He smirked. "What about money?"

"How do you make a lot of it?"

"Why do you want to know?"

"I don't know. Maybe it'll help me be happy and free?"

"I doubt it. I know a lot of unhappy rich people."

"True, but—"

"Your problem is you link money to your self-worth," Mark interrupted. "But money is just a vehicle for something else, like the freedom to travel or take advantage of opportunities."

"I want that!"

"Then earn it. Follow the five steps in creating a world. There are no shortcuts to it. If you try to shortcut, you will short-circuit. Did I ever tell you the bank robber story?"

Mark began to tell it to me:

There was a Twilight Zone *episode called "A Nice Place to Visit" about a bank robber who died and was awakened by an angel.*

"Hello, Mr. Bank Robber, we've been expecting you," the angel says. "What can I do for you?"

"Am I dead?" asks the bank robber.

"Yes. I'm your angel and am at your service."

"Like I can ask for wishes or something?"

"Yes."

"Okay. Then I want food, lots of it."

"As you wish."

The bank robber is treated to a meal fit for kings. He notices that since he's dead, he can keep on eating and eating to his delight.

"Angel," the bank robber says. "I'm tired of the food. I want women, lots of women."

"Very well," says the angel.

The bank robber has romantic affairs with countless women, and since he is dead, these encounters continue indefinitely. But the bank robber grows sad.

"What's wrong?" asks the angel.

"I appreciate the food and the company, but I'm bored. I miss being alive. I want to rob a bank!"

"I can arrange that."

A bank appears out of nowhere. The bank robber is pleased and excited. He enters the bank and is warmly greeted by the bank manager. "Mr. Bank Robber, we are so happy to have you visit us. We have prepared all our money in tidy bags so it will be easy for you to steal. Please, take whatever you like."

The bank robber is devastated. "Angel, the food, women, and the bank. It's all too much. I don't belong here in heaven. Please send me to the other place!"

The angel responds, "Where do you think you are? This is the other place."

"Kid, it's the journey, not the destination," Mark had said, his eyes alight. "It's not about the result or the money. It's about the ups and downs, the battles, the experiences that will bring you happiness and peace. Maintain your focus and trust the Process."

Back in my hotel room, I shut my eyes tight and downed the rest of my second beer. My focus *had* been on the money. I loved seeing that number in my bank account get higher and higher. That number felt like freedom, security, and happiness for myself and my family. But it was like eating forever without getting full, like trying to rob a bank with no resistance—a hollow victory, and never enough to satisfy.

A *vehicle for something else*, Mark said about money. But I was wandering along on the side of the road, missing every ride that passed me by, fixated on the weeds and rocks. I was missing opportunities to really connect with the people I advised, with the people who loved me. I went to grab my third beer.

Like what always happened after I started drinking, some of my worst memories drifted into sharp focus. In the background of my vision, I saw a young male newscaster standing in a Syrian town square, updating the audience on the gruesome details of the civil war. But in the foreground, I saw my mother looking gaunt and pale in a hospital bed. And my dog Mordi's body softening into Heather's arms in our vet's office.

* * *

In 2014, Mordi, our beloved dog, was unexpectedly diagnosed with kidney failure at only ten years old. The vet had said he only had at most two months to live. Our little Jack Russell with the brown prayer cap was beginning to stand up more slowly, get less excited for walks, and turn his nose up at his food. We had to give him daily saline solution infusions, and he was on a special diet and all kinds of meds. It was devastating for all of us.

While I was in town one morning, I brought Mordi to the vet to see about his fluids. Dr. John, a kind man with a young-looking face to match his optimistic personality, said he'd lost weight, so they would keep him there to observe him. I went home, but then only a few hours later, Dr. John called and told me Mordi was very sick, and disoriented, and his blood work was poor. He had lost weight and was anemic. It was time for him to go. He was suffering so much, and I knew Dr. John was right.

Heather and I drove together to the vet, leaving Zachary at my father's house. In his kennel, Mordi looked so uncomfortable and weak. When we took him out and put him on the floor, he wagged his tail but didn't kiss or lick anyone. I couldn't stop crying. I picked him up again and carried him to the room.

"We'll find each other soon," I told him. "I love you so much. I'll see you real soon."

They put Mordi on a metal table and gave him a liquid via needle. I had to step out of the room as I was so upset. Heather stayed with him and held him as he took his last breath. Within a few seconds, it was over, and he passed away peacefully in her arms.

When we picked up Zachary and made it home, Heather and I held each other for a long time. Then we meditated together, both crying hard and feeling him in our hearts.

Hours later, I was still crying, so I went onto my back porch and called Mark.

"He was only ten years old," I said. "It's not fair. But this is the dark side, right? I must be insane."

"No, you're not insane," Mark said.

"This is just a drama, right?"

"No, Alex. You're human."

I paused. I'd expected him to have some clever response or to point out something I could improve, but he didn't. I felt my breathing slow down as I allowed myself to feel the full weight of this pain.

"It hurts, Mark. Seeing him like that was one of the worst experiences in my life."

"I know. I've lost dogs. My wife won't let us get dogs anymore. It's too painful for her."

"You're so strong. You must not even cry."

"Of course I do. I cried when I lost my dogs. They're incredible animals."

"So what should I do?"

"Instead of focusing completely on the pain of the loss, I choose to focus on the wonderful times I had with my dogs. They wouldn't want me to feel unhappy. They would want me to be happy because that is their nature. But it won't happen overnight. You're grieving, Alex. Give yourself some time."

I sighed deeply as I remembered this conversation. Lying on the hotel bed, the room now completely dark except for a single lamp, I smiled, imagining Mordi bounding through our backyard, his little legs kicking out like miniature pistons, his body a white blur. And I imagined him trotting toward me, his pink tongue sticking out and dark eyes full of life. Strangely, the lamp kept flickering for no apparent reason. What else had Mark said at that time? I strained to remember, then it came to me.

"What do you think about death, Mark?" I had asked him.

"I don't think about it," he said simply.

"Why not?"

"I can't do anything about it. It will happen to me and to everyone and everything I love."

"You don't think it's sad?"

"When I'm old and can't do much, and my body grows weak, it will be a welcome blessing."

"What do you think happens when we die?" I asked.

"I believe what the Process teaches: that our essence continues."

"But if it's not true, so what? If your soul doesn't continue, then all is lost. All meaning is gone."

"You'll live on, even if the soul doesn't continue."

"How is that possible?"

"I'll live on in you," Mark said. "The teachings I've given you, they will continue. All the people I've helped and touched, I'm a part of them. My essence is perpetuated in the hearts and minds of those I love and care for, and for the difference I have made in this world. Even my atoms will make up new beings and materials. In the same way, Mordi lives on in you, through all the wonderful memories you have of him. There is no end to that."

The hotel lamp light flickered again, jolting me out of my reverie. I put my head in my hands. What was it that was living on through me? My absence from my family? Running away from myself? Putting on a façade to help others? I pushed the thoughts away, like I'd gotten so good at doing, and tried remembering what I'd said next to my uncle.

"Sometimes I can't help but worry about death," I'd said.

"Dark side," Mark said simply. "That's pain with no benefit. I can share with you this additional insight that may comfort you, nephew," he said. "Your fear of death will diminish when you live a life you are proud of and at peace with. By the way, have you ever heard the story of the wise monk?"

He told me the story:

There was once a young monk who asked a wise monk, "What happens when we die?"

"How should I know?" the wise monk said.

"Because you're a master."

The wise monk responded, "But I'm not a dead one."

Mark continued, "It's all a mystery, kid. You have to live your life in the here and now, as best you can. Concern yourself with things you are able to influence and make the world around you better. But to do that, you have to be strong. So first things first: Take care of yourself, Alex. Go be with your family."

Be strong. Take care of yourself. Go be with your family. These were obvious solutions, especially since I believed in the Process so strongly and witnessed all it had blessed me with. All Mark had blessed me with. But now all I seemed to be able to focus on was work, work, work. Maybe I was afraid of how fragile and unpredictable life was, and I wanted to build my walls high enough. As if I could protect myself. But of course, I could only do what I could do and had to let go of the rest. I decided to have a fourth beer before thinking about *that* experience again.

But after I drank half the can and turned off the flickering lamp, I fell asleep on top of the covers without brushing my teeth or calling Heather to say good night.

* * *

I woke up at eight the next morning feeling bloated and groggy. In the bathroom mirror, the dark circles under my eyes looked like pools of gray wax. I started brushing my teeth when a memory came back to me in a flash.

"The Intensive!" I said out loud, the toothbrush hanging out of my mouth. "*The Intensive!*"

All those years ago, Mark had mentioned something he called an Intensive—a deeper dive into the Process itself. Where the real you is revealed. An experience that has to change you by the nature of its sheer potency. Maybe that was what I needed—something I couldn't look away from—to help me become the person I was meant to be. I figured Mark was already at work and immediately called his office.

The receptionist put me in touch with him.

"Alex!" he boomed. "I haven't heard from you in a while. How you been?"

"I've been good, good. Listen, I'm going to be in town this weekend. Can we meet up sometime on Friday? There's something I need to ask you."

"Sounds serious. All right, come on over. We'll make dinner."

CHAPTER 8

* * *

Desperate Times

You can't connect the dots looking forward; you can only connect them looking backwards. So, you have to trust that the dots will somehow connect in your future.

—Steve Jobs

When I pulled into Mark's driveway Friday evening, the garage door was open and Mark was at his worktable, filling his supplement jars, same as ever. He was wearing an orange Syracuse sweatshirt and worn jeans. I got out of the car and stood there watching him for a few minutes, anxiously switching from foot to foot while he finished up. I was already sweating through the khaki dress pants and white button-up I was wearing under the early-April sun still haunting the sky. Though the lines in Mark's face had gotten slightly deeper over the past decade, and his hair was now completely gray, his energy hadn't diminished a bit since I'd first met him.

Finally, he wiped his hands with a towel and patted my shoulder. "Good to see you, Alex. It's been a while."

"Good to see you too, Mark. Really good."

He looked at me intently. "Did you take your wheatgrass before coming?"

"Yes, I did."

"How about your walk and meditation?"

"I didn't wake up early enough for anything else."

"But you were on the computer all day?"

I blushed. "Okay, yeah, I worked instead of getting balanced."

Mark smiled. "I can see that. It's all over your face. I would tell you to go meditate, but let's save that for later. How about a cup of tea?"

When he went to make the tea for us, I circled the garage, remembering all the time I'd spent here. The place was as cluttered as always with towering storage shelves overflowing with papers and baskets and bins. But it still felt like home. That same soothing energy still permeated everything.

On a wall above the worktable, I found something new: a framed photo showing Mark, Heather, and me at our wedding. Mark was in his three-piece suit, his eyes wide open as if he was taking in some vast landscape. Heather wore her strapless wedding dress with her skin freshly tanned, and I had a goatee rather than the full stubble beard I had now.

Even though our smiles were put on for the camera, happiness clearly radiated from us.

At the reception, Mark had given a speech from his position as Heather's and my guide. One part of Mark's speech had stuck with me after all this time: "A wise sage was asked to tell the secret of the Bible on one leg. He said, 'Love thy neighbor as thyself. All the rest is commentary.'" He'd then explained that Heather and I were each other's closest neighbors, so the commandment applied even more strictly to us.

Mark had taught me that making the world around me better made my world better, but was I doing that? I thought about each sector of my life: my work, my wife and son, my extended family, my friends, my personal health, my core values. All I was attending to with gusto was work, and sure, I'd seen our business improve others' lives. But what about everything else? This anxiety, this self-focus, was pulling me away from so much that was important to me, and I was done with it. I wanted to love my neighbors, every one of them, and make a difference in the lives of those around me. And I knew exactly where to begin.

Mark came in with two mugs—one with a cartoon map of New York City on it, and one a plain black mug with "my cup of sanity" in hand-painted cursive on the side—and placed them on the coffee table. He sat down and turned toward me. "So, Alex, what can I do you for?"

I took a deep breath. "I haven't been doing too well lately."

"Something wrong with the business?"

"Not exactly . . ."

"With your marriage?"

"No, we're doing pretty . . ."

"Are you using the Tools?"

I rolled my eyes and motioned toward my body. "I think you know the answer to that. Honestly, I've been self-medicating."

"I wondered about that."

"Drinking and overeating. It's gotten worse lately."

"When you don't use the Tools, you'll find other tools that leave you worse off. You have to be clean."

"I shower every day," I joked.

Mark smiled. "Think of *clean* as synonymous with the light, and *dirty* as the dark. Being clean is a lot of things: not manipulating, doing the right thing. But it's also avoiding substances that cause you to be less vigilant. The dark side is always looking for a chance to pounce, and it's beginning to win you over now. You have to guard yourself against it."

"So you're telling me to avoid these substances entirely? I don't know if I can do that."

"Of course you can!" Mark raised his arms in the air. "You're human. You're not an animal. You're in control, Alex. Remember the pain amplifier. It sounds like you're trapping yourself in there again."

"Yeah, maybe. I just . . ."

I remembered the woman who'd come up to me after the talk I'd given. How much I'd helped her, yet how much of a fraud I still felt.

"I know this is a crazy question," I started. "But what is my purpose? Why am I here?"

"To be God," he said.

"You're going to have to explain that more," I told him.

"To be God is to be a creator. Your purpose is to receive light in order to share it. Light can be what I've taught you. You receive the benefits, and now you share them with others, thus improving their world."

"Making the world around me better, to make my world better?" I questioned.

"That's right. You realize we're all one, the same energy. Therefore, you have this mirror effect I taught you. What you do for others comes back to you."

"But what about making money and achieving things? Can that be part of my purpose?"

"Sure, money is a form of energy. You get it and then you share it."

"So it's better to give than to receive?" This thought comforted me, like maybe I didn't *need* to worry so much about improving myself and my health. Maybe what I was doing for others could be enough. But Mark quickly quashed that idea.

"You can't give what you don't have. I've taught you how to create worlds. I taught you magic. I taught you the Process. You have the power. You will receive abundance. Enjoy the abundance and share it. Otherwise, you will short-circuit. You'll invite the dark side in. You can't hold on to the light. It only works by sharing. Then, you will feel connected and not lonely."

"Does it make sense for me to be afraid of the dark side?" I asked Mark. "Shouldn't I run away from it and toward the good?"

"No," he responded. "Just be aware the dark side is there. Don't feed it. Even fearing it is feeding it. Running away from it is feeding it. You're giving it undue power when you indulge it. This is what I call 'praying to the dark side.'"

"Can it be healed?"

"It's not a question of being healed. The things that activate it can be healed, like the pain that triggers it. But it will always be there, waiting, even if you've overcome the old triggers."

"So the dark side is bad, then?"

"It's not good or bad, per se. It's like the fable of the scorpion and the frog. The scorpion convinces the frog to carry him across the river, but midway, he stings the frog, dooming them both. When the frog asks why, the scorpion says, 'Because it's my nature.' The dark side is the same. Its nature is to obscure the light. It isn't personal. It is just its nature."

"But you said good is light and evil is dark."

"Yes, that's how we experience it on this plane of existence. But darkness is simply the absence of light. What happens when you inject light into a dark room?"

"The room is lit up," I said.

Mark nodded. "The darkness recedes. So the answer to overcome darkness is to add light."

I crossed my arms over my chest and asked, "So what's even the point of darkness? Why couldn't everything just be light all the time? The world would be so much better."

Mark smiled good-naturedly, just like he had when I was younger asking him about black holes. He took a slow sip of his tea before beginning.

"Dark gives us a choice. Without the dark, we would simply be overwhelmed by light and have no free will. If we get light and have not earned it, we suffer.

"To earn the light, we must transform the desire to receive selfishly to the desire to receive in order to share. And through sharing you are given the opportunity to be a creator."

I repeated the last sentence in my mind: *And through sharing you are given the opportunity to be a creator.*

"Do you know the dark's greatest weapon?" Mark asked.

"I have no idea," I said.

"Doubt."

"I wouldn't have guessed that."

"You've seen how the world works," Mark said patiently. "I taught you the Process. I gave you the Tools. Yet you still make the same mistakes. You still go into drama."

My shoulders slumped. "It's true. All the things you taught me make my life better, but I still do get pulled into fear and drama. I can't believe I'm still doing it."

"All of that is the dark, built into the game of life. Until you change the programming you have, it's easy to slip back. The object of the game is to get better and better. It doesn't all happen at once. It takes time to develop the new programs."

I couldn't help but wonder how long it would take me. When would the new program take hold? How long had it taken Mark? As many years as it would take me?

"How do I doubt less?" I asked.

"You don't. Doubt will come. It's training you. Each time you overcome doubt with trust, your trust grows stronger. Each time you give in to doubt, doubt becomes stronger. It's like exercise. You exercise your trust and certainty to build that muscle."

Like exercise. When I stopped training in the Process, my doubt became stronger than my trust and certainty. It was so obvious. And I knew then, with everything in me, that I was taking the correct next step.

"Mark, I want to do an Intensive."

He raised an eyebrow at me, clearly taken by surprise, but I barreled forward to hopefully get ahead of his skepticism.

"You told me about it years ago. You said you didn't think I'd need to go through it, that you wanted to teach me everything I needed to know. But I'm desperate, Mark. I want to go deeper. I want to know my dark side and overcome it."

He looked at me incredulously. "Desperate? Just use the Tools. Remember that the magic is your perception and act accordingly. You don't want to see your dark side. It ain't pretty."

That was always his response: Use the Tools. They'll remind you that the world is an illusion, it's made of magic, and the magic is perception. And of course, those teachings were invaluable to me. They were the reason both Heather and I were where we were. But everything had its limit. Should I be ashamed to want more, all that the Process had to give? All it had given Mark? I didn't think so.

"The wheatgrass is easy enough," I said. "I try to meditate and take walks. I try to remember that I create my world. But something in me just won't be touched. I feel completely overwhelmed. I'm not there for my family like I need to be. I'm stuck in my dramas. I'm not staying clean."

"Okay, but you're here. You can still change. There is no failure, Alex. Each setback, which you may call a failure, is a learning opportunity. You make adjustments and start a new adventure."

"Exactly, and that's what I need your help with. My next adventure is the Intensive. I just know it."

Mark sighed deeply and leaned forward to pick up his tea. Hands clasped around the mug, he closed his eyes and breathed in the steam, then took a small sip. With his eyes still shut, he said, "You're not in the right state of mind for that. You can't go deeper when you're already insane—you'll just find more insanity. Trust me on that."

"Of course I trust you. But I know this is what I need."

"You might see something you're not ready to see." He opened his eyes. There was a sheen over them. "When I did my first Intensive, Ed took me to an island in the Bahamas. The facilitators brought a small group of us into a room and put a crystal in the middle of our circle. Once they'd led us into a meditation, the facilitators said:

Now imagine that crystal building up energy. Now imagine that energy going from the crystal to your central core. Now imagine that energy going from that central core through your heart up into your head.

"And as it went through my heart, all of a sudden I saw what I was doing to myself to achieve what I'd achieved. I saw how I had hurt that child within me. I would always have to say, 'Shut up, Mark. Shut up, don't open your mouth, you'll get me in trouble.' Being a doctor, my happy-go-lucky kid had to be shut off in order to do what I had to do to get to where I had to get to.

"When I saw that little inner child, I broke down. I said to him, 'Oh my God, look what I've done to you. I'm never gonna let that happen again.' But if I hadn't been ready, if I hadn't been following the Process, if I hadn't been aware of what I was getting into, then that realization could've messed me up. If I'd been afraid, it could've broken me to see what I saw. To know that was in there and to not know what to do about it."

I leaned forward with my elbows on my knees. That was exactly what I wanted—to know what was at the central core of me, what I was trying to avoid, what was preventing me from being the man I wanted to be. I wanted to throw light into every dark corner of myself. I had to be ready for that for my life to get back on track.

"I want that, Mark. I'll do whatever I have to do to get there. I'll take off work starting today. I'll stay in the Bahamas with you for as long as necessary. Whatever."

Mark laughed. "You do know I have a life of my own. Patients and my own family, etcetera. And we wouldn't have to go to the Bahamas. I could lead you through a session here, in the same room you always meditate in. But you're not ready for it." Suddenly, Mark put his hands on his knees and stood up. "I'm going to go help Nice finish up dinner."

"Wait." I stood up with him. "I'm going to do this either way. Maybe I'll go on a retreat with a guru or shaman. I'll do it anyway, with or without you."

"And that's your decision. Alex, I can't read your mind or see your thoughts. I can't know your intentions."

"You're right, you can't. You just have to trust me."

Mark stared at me for a few moments, then sighed deeply. "I wanted you to do it the easy way, use the Tools, but you're insisting on doing it the hard way. You don't have to see the things I had to see. You're impatient. You don't need to do that."

"But—"

"But," Mark interrupted me, "I can tell you're serious. So maybe I'm wrong. Maybe you have to experience your dark side, same as me. I just don't want you to suffer. I'm trying to protect you from this. Maybe I'm being too much of your uncle here." He paused and then continued. "But I don't blame you. I wanted to see, and so do you. Just know that whatever happens, it's your responsibility. And you have a family to think about. Remember that and take it seriously."

"I *have*—"

Mark held up a hand. "Really think about it. Then we'll talk."

He spun around and disappeared into the house.

I knew what I had to do. I needed to prove to myself that I could confront my reality on my own, that I could see whatever I would see in the depths of my psyche without being overwhelmed or breaking. He was right: All I was doing now was escaping. I wasn't staying clean, taking responsibility for my perception, or using the Tools. The Intensive couldn't be an extension of that, or it might be devastating.

I headed to my old meditation room in Mark's house and sat on the same full-sized bed where I'd first learned to meditate. The sun just barely cast its light through the closed curtains behind the headboard, filling the room with a hazy orange glow. With some effort, I closed my eyes and tuned in to the sounds around me, and I paid attention to the clipped beat of my heart. Then I set an intention, as simple and straightforward as I could make it:

Show me what I'm avoiding. I'm ready to see it.

For a while, nothing changed. The air conditioner hummed, the muffled sounds of clinking silverware and dishes clattering on stone countertops drifted through the walls, and the cicadas cried outside the window. Still, I stayed with my intention.

Then, like a movie reel flickering to life, I found myself in a hotel room with Heather on a business trip in Vegas we'd taken last year. I heard my cell phone ring and saw that it was Rose, my mother's neighbor, who told me that she couldn't get a hold of my mother. She wanted to know if I'd heard from her. I told Rose I hadn't spoken to my mother in weeks, but that wasn't too uncommon—she often fell off the face of the earth for long periods of time. Still, Rose had a bad feeling. And the more we talked, so did I.

Like an instinct, I opened my eyes and snapped out of the memory. I started wondering what kind of booze Mark had in the house. He probably had some rum at least, and maybe I'd ask for some with my dinner. A rum and Diet Coke. Perfect. Just a little something to . . .

But that was the dark side, I told myself. I willed myself to remember my intention: *Show me what I'm avoiding. I'm ready to see it.*

In my mind, I heard the phone ring again. Rose. She was beside herself, crying, trying to tell me in between sobs that she'd found my mother face down on the carpet, passed out from an apparent overdose. She told me the ambulance was on its way and for us to get down there as soon as we could.

Seeing my mother like that, gaunt and wild-haired in the hospital bed, knowing that I'd been supporting her while she actively harmed herself, knowing that I hadn't done everything I could to prevent it from happening . . . I didn't want to face it. I didn't want to face the guilt, the disappointment, that image of her so helpless and exhausted.

And now, I had to realize that I didn't want to face the part of me that she represented, maybe even more so. I didn't want to acknowledge that my desire to escape was the same as hers, even if the materials were different: She zoned out to the TV; I worked a hundred hours a week. She took pills and injected drugs; I drank or distracted myself till my mind shut off and I could finally sleep. My mother's addiction was her way of escaping the pain and trauma she'd experienced in her life, just as I had been trying to escape mine.

Mark always said, "When the Higher Self speaks, there are no more questions." And without a doubt, I saw how my own choices were leading me down a path that was all too similar to my mother's. The thought was almost unbearable, but I forced myself to stay with it.

Waves of remorse flowed through me. Anger at my situation. Disappointment in my mother and in myself. These emotions coiled up in my chest, tightened my stomach, and made my arms hurt. And then, after I don't know how long, these powerful, stagnant emotions began to flow. They were still uncomfortable and painful, but they were no longer stuck in my body—it was like I'd broken a dam, allowing debris-filled water to rush through me. In a way, and if only for a moment, I felt free of the compulsion to run away. I felt okay being with what I was feeling. At least, more okay than I had before.

I decided to sit in meditation for a while longer to regain my balance. After avoiding myself for weeks, meditation helped me feel calmer, more clearheaded, and more energetic. Once my heart had returned to its normal rhythm, I got up and headed to the dining room to join Mark and Nice.

"I know this is the right next step for me, Mark," I said as I sat down beside him. "And I take full responsibility for whatever happens afterward."

Mark nodded. "Okay."

"Okay?" I repeated, hopeful.

Mark nodded. "Okay. Your agency is everything, Alex. I will lead you in an Intensive."

My heart started racing, but I did my best to still it. "Thank you. Thank you."

Mark said, "We can do it tomorrow. Remember that Saturday is when the universe's energy is greatest. There's no better time to connect deeply with Source."

My heart leaped. "Absolutely."

"Okay. I'll make the preparations tonight. I have synagogue in the morning, so come over any time after noon tomorrow."

I tried to contain my excitement. I felt like dancing, like singing. Finally, my life was about to get back on track. I was about to grow that much closer to the man I was always supposed to be. I could hardly wait.

"Tonight," Mark said between bites, "think about the intention you want to set for our session."

"Already have one," I said.

"Well, let's hear it."

"I want to face my fears—fully."

Mark raised his eyebrows. "I have a feeling you will be getting exactly that."

CHAPTER 9

* * *

The Intensive

End? No, the journey doesn't end here. Death is just another path . . . One that we all must take.

—Gandalf, *The Lord of the Rings: The Return of the King* (2003 film)

The next day, I pulled into Mark's driveway at 1 PM on the dot. Nice answered the door and quietly led me toward the meditation room. But instead of going there, she opened another door across the hall.

It was small and plain with hardwood floors, with a few photos of Mark and Nice hanging up and a brown leather couch against the wall where Mark sat, his legs crossed and his eyes closed. He looked like a kindly hermit: old brown sweatshirt, black sweatpants, serene expression. The lights were off, though the stubborn Florida sunlight filtered through the curtains as always.

In the middle of the floor was something like a pallet—quilted blankets stacked on top of each other and a blue pillow with a black sleeping mask lying on it.

Nice put her hand against my back. "Put on the mask and lie down on the blankets. Mark will tell you what to do next. I'll be here if either of you need anything."

I smiled at her as she closed the door, then did as she said. I lay there with my hands clasped on my stomach, my eyes masked, waiting for Mark to say something.

Mark took a deep breath before speaking. "Alex, welcome. This session will last two hours unless you feel it's natural to continue for longer, or if you want to stop earlier. I'll walk you through the basics as we go on. But that will only be an entry point. The real journey will come afterward, and I'll lead you through that too."

"I'm ready," I said.

"Wonderful. I'll see you on the other side." I heard a smile in Mark's voice, and then he was silent.

A few moments later, I heard in my mind what sounded like binaural beats, long instances of one note, layered many times over, with great depth. It sounded like being underwater and hearing the low bellow of a boat's horn. I wasn't sure if Mark was playing something, or I was just imagining it.

Mark invited me to tune in to my breathing the same way I'd done hundreds of times before. I listened to my surroundings: this internal music, sparrows chirping outside the window, air conditioner humming. I observed the sensations in my body: tightness in my throat, in my chest, and slight nausea. The constant seed of anxiety—a tight knot—waiting in my stomach.

"Begin breathing only through your mouth," Mark instructed.

I felt the cold air in the room pass over my tongue and down my throat with each big breath in. Thoughts came and went—about Heather, about Zachary, about my mother, about the work I'd have to catch up on come Monday, and would I be in a good space to do that? I used my training to allow each thought to pass without fixating it or judging myself for it. Slowly, I began to relax more and more, as if sinking into the floor.

Suddenly my hands began to tingle. I felt an intense openness piercing my chest. This was the same euphoria I'd experienced before in meditation. But then other emotions moved through me, some of them less comfortable, so intertwined with each other that they were hard to tease out.

My arms started tensing, my hands felt frozen, and my neck seized up. I grew afraid of where this was headed. But I trusted Mark and reminded myself of my intention. I knew this wouldn't be easy.

The longer I stuck with the technique and the sensations, the more alive I felt. I laughed every so often. Without thinking, I rolled from side to side like a child playing. I was open and responsive, full of energy that was being freed up from months of suppression.

"Now slowly return your breathing to normal." Mark's voice sounded twice as slow as it had when we'd begun.

I began to breathe more slowly and soon fell into a

trancelike state, somewhere between waking and sleep where I was only slightly aware of my body. It felt like breathing nitrogen gas at the dentist's office, dreamy and easy.

Mark's voice sounded like it was everywhere. "Now, Alex, go where you need to go."

* * *

You know how in time-traveling movies, there's that moment where the main character is ripped from the present into some kind of time-vortex tunnel? Where stripes of color zoom past them, and they're terrified and disoriented? That's what it felt like to be pulled headfirst into an all-consuming space in my psyche where fear was all I could feel.

Suddenly, I was no longer in that small room in Mark and Nice's house. It was like I'd stepped through a hole in the ground and was now falling, falling, falling, farther and farther down into the dark. Stripes of dark earth streamed past my vision. I didn't know where I was or where I was going, but somehow I seemed to be zooming through the planet itself. I screamed, digging my fingernails into the earth in front of me, grasping at twiggy roots and small white bones and loose stones that all gave way and fell with me. I looked up and saw an ever-shrinking circle of light. I knew I was going to die. I *knew* I would die.

"Mark! Mark! Get Heather!" I shrieked.

"You're okay." Mark's voice pervaded everything, like I was underwater.

"I don't want to die!"

"Say the *Sh'ma Yisrael,*" he commanded, directing me to the Jewish prayer from Deuteronomy 6:4–9 in the Torah. "And let go."

Air whooshed past me. I didn't dare look down. I closed my eyes and recited the prayer, so familiar to me from services I'd attended, my voice shaking: "*Sh'ma Yisrael, Adonai Eloheinu, Adonai Echad!* Hear, O Israel, the Lord our God, the Lord is One!"

I recited the prayer a dozen times, then a dozen more, still impossibly falling farther downward. When I next opened my eyes, the tunnel had become much wider. The wall of earth was at least ten feet away from me. A cloud of dirt and bones and stones surrounded me like planets around a dying sun.

In between the words of the prayer, I heard a raspy voice cackling near me. It said, "Mark told you that you didn't need this. Now you're going to die or go crazy."

The voice terrified me. I didn't want to see what or whom it belonged to. I continued reciting the prayer, tightly shutting my eyes.

"What was the point, Alex?" The voice was sinister and cutting. "You thought this would feel good, didn't you? You never actually wanted to get better; you just wanted to *feel good.* Feel more important. Feel more interesting. Feel more high. But instead, you're just going to lose your mind. When will you learn, Alex?"

I screamed again, a primal guttural cry, flailing like mad

to find something to hold on to. But I was helpless. There was only the air around me, the ever-growing tunnel of dark earth, and my desperate screams. I knew I was going to die, and I was afraid of it.

"Mark, I can't . . ."

"The only way out is through," Mark's voice bellowed. "The only way out is through."

Through, I repeated in some part of my terrified brain. *The only way out . . .*

Finally, I understood. I stopped screaming. I let go of the prayer and allowed the critical voice to fill the space around me: "You're nothing. You're hopeless. Why are you even here?" On and on it went, and I let the words pass over me like water. I stopped resisting it all, allowing my entire body to surrender to the fall, to the fear.

After a few moments, the tunnel began to brighten up. The walls around me grew closer, shrinking in diameter, until I could almost reach out and touch them. I looked down and noticed a circle of light had appeared at the bottom of this deep, dark hole, and that I was rushing toward it. I began to lose sight of myself, of who I was, of who *Alex* was. It should've been scary, but it wasn't. It felt like shedding a too-old skin. I felt like something nameless and blank being pulled through this world with no will of its own. And before I knew it, *whoever I was* was passing through that blinding light into a space on the other side.

My body landed roughly on something thick and soft. My fingers brushed over it—a shag carpet. There was the old boxy TV, the yellow wallpaper, the big picture window. I was in the living room at my parents' old house, before they'd built the one Dad lived in now. I pulled my hands up in front of my face. They were almost as small as a baby's. I crawled over to the TV and watched bright-colored cartoon characters bobbing around on the screen, which got me laughing. I rolled to the wall and tried to stick my fingers in the electrical socket, but a big hand stopped me, and it made me laugh more. I wanted a hug and was pulled in by someone warm and kind with a deep voice. The man told me he loved me, and it made warmth spread through my chest. Then I was alone again, and I didn't mind that either.

In that room from my youth, I experienced no distinction between minutes or days. I found myself alone but didn't feel lonely. With the TV, my blocks, the carpet, and my own small self, I seemed to have all I needed. I didn't want for anything or even remember what there had been to want.

I didn't even remember who I was. I didn't remember anything. What a joy it was—to forget.

* * *

". . . Come back, Alex. You're out of it now. Breathe slowly. Come back."

I opened my eyes and saw only blackness. My heart started pounding. Had I lost my vision? Then Mark slipped off the sleeping mask I'd forgotten I was wearing.

The room was dim now with only a small lamp glowing

on the dresser. I wanted to sit up but wasn't sure I could move. My hands felt frozen, and my forearms burned.

"Breathe deeply," Mark said from beside me. "It's okay. I've got you."

I took some time to steady my breathing and calm myself down. I wanted to ask questions or say something, but the words wouldn't come. My throat felt dry, but I noticed it was no longer tight.

"The session lasted longer than I expected," Mark began. "Three hours. Your energy was strong. I saw you transform, Alex. You went through an existential struggle where you prevailed and were reborn. I saw a hunk of clay being shaped into something new and beautiful. You wanted the truth, and you got the truth!"

"What happened?" I finally managed to ask.

He knelt down and gripped my shoulder. "Take your time. Don't intellectualize this or overthink it. You won't fully understand it through your Middle Self. When you're ready, we can talk about how it felt."

I tried to sit up on my elbows, but the effort felt massive.

"Don't get up yet," Mark said. "Rest here a while and process. I'll be outside when you're ready."

He soundlessly rose and closed the door behind him.

I lay there and allowed my breathing to slow. The terrifying fall felt like a distant memory. What prevailed now was a sense of complete wonder. When I glanced around the room, everything looked new and beautiful. The light from the lamp looked like a liquid flowing through the air, and the white paint on the walls looked bright and happy. I let out one laugh, then another, then another, getting louder and louder with each. I placed one hand on my belly and another on my chest and reveled in this connection and joy. For minutes I stayed like that, overwhelmed with lightness and a sense of freedom from all my old stories.

After the life returned to my limbs, I rolled onto my side and pressed myself up to stand. I saw myself in a small mirror hung up on the wall and noticed a bright halo of white light surrounding me.

I walked toward the mirror and touched it. I'd once seen myself as a sad, small kid agonizing over dramas he had no control over. I imagined him as he looked the day I'd first meditated at Mark's house. Then I imagined a much older version of myself, deep wrinkles crossing my forehead and cheeks, a gray beard, and thin lips. For the first time, I didn't wish away this older man, but I loved him. I knew I'd be proud to be him one day, just like I was proud of that kid who'd been doing his best.

I looked at myself in the mirror for a long time. All of these iterations of me said at once nothing about who I was and everything about what my journey on this earth was supposed to mean. I was once a young, helpless boy. I was once a heartbroken dreamer who didn't know how to manage the demands of the world. I was now a man with a family, one who was confronting his vices and doubt. And one day, perhaps I would be an old man who wanted nothing more than to look back at all of this, in his silent and reflective moments, and know that he did the best he could.

To tell you the truth, by that point, I wasn't sure who I was. And what a relief it was to be nobody.

* * *

I found Mark in the living room, meditating on the couch.

"So? How do you feel?" he asked when I sat down next to him.

"I feel strange. I'm not sure how to describe it."

Mark smiled. "You'll come back to yourself. You faced your fear of death head-on. It will take a while to reintegrate."

"I finally realize how afraid I am," I said. "How deep the roots go. Letting go was almost impossible. I don't want to go back to that."

Mark raised an eyebrow at me. "How did it feel to let go?"

"Incredible. I feel like a new person, like I was reborn. But the journey there was . . ."

"Horrifying, right?" Mark's smile was comically big, and it made me laugh. "I tried to take it easy on you. I wanted to teach you everything, so you didn't have to go through what I did. But you know what? Maybe you have to do things the hard way. Sometimes the hard way is the only way."

"And what was with that voice? The one taunting me? Was it my inner critic?"

"I don't use that terminology. What you're referring to comes from a program. Just like we talked about, how when you were born you were put in a cage, and you developed this program of inferiority. Because of this program, you beat up on yourself."

"Is it my dark side?"

"Yep. It's pain with no benefit.

"How do I just let it go?"

"It's not about letting it go, per se. You must become aware of what's going on." Mark continued, "This session was the start. Now, it's your job to recognize when it's taking over, use the Tools, and say S-T-O-P. Know you're in control of it. You don't have to let it rule you."

I nodded. That was exactly what had helped me out of these ruts before.

Despite the terror I'd felt, the overwhelming sensation was how incredible the world looked around me. The blue sky outside the window stunned me. I couldn't stop smiling.

Then an image of my mother in her hospital bed reappeared to me.

I recalled how when she'd first woken up after the overdose, she was disoriented. She didn't recognize me, Heather, or Zachary. But after a few days, once she'd regained her senses, she was like a new person. Happier, more outgoing, more talkative. She initiated plans with Heather and me while before, she'd cancel on us constantly, and she asked to have Zachary over all the time. She even remodeled her walk-in closet to be a bedroom for him, complete with a little bed that looked like a spaceship and a wooden sign with his name painted on it.

But the most incredible moment happened while we were walking around the Jungle Island Zoo in Miami. Mom was still in a wheelchair after her hospital stay, but her spirits were high as I wheeled her over the pavement between the enclosures. As we passed the orangutan exhibit, Mom asked if we could stop.

Two of the older orangutans, a male and a female, with their shaggy orange fur and wrinkly faces, were eating bananas while a young orangutan hung from a tree branch by one arm, its dark eyes surveying us. My mother watched them for a long time, seemingly entranced.

I bent down to get on her level and nodded at the enclosure. "What do you like about them?"

Her hazel-green eyes were shining. "I don't know. They just make me happy."

The young orangutan was now hanging upside down from the branch, swiping its hand at the older female. She played along, grunting dramatically with every swipe. When the little one dropped from the branch and ran away, she chased it.

"They look so much like us," my mother continued. "But they're so much sillier too. Maybe they have the right idea. Maybe it's time for me to grow out my hair and run around naked. Or at least eat more bananas."

We both laughed. I reached out to rub her arm. "It's great seeing you like this, Mom."

"Oh, don't get sappy on me now."

"I'm serious. Don't you feel different?"

"I do. Things feel easier. My mind's clearer. You know, when I really think about it, I'm not sure I've ever been this happy." She looked up at me and a quick gasp escaped her. She suddenly began to cry. "Oh, I'm afraid of going back. I don't want to go back to how it was. I don't know if I can . . ."

Heather knelt down and hugged her. "Breathe. It's okay. Breathe."

My mother brought a hand up to grab Heather's arm, breathing deeply with her eyes closed. They stayed like that for a few minutes. Zachary was running along the fence, making noises and faces at the orangutans.

"I love you guys," my mother said finally, still crying. "My beautiful kiddos. My family."

It was incredible to see her like that, so full of life and love after a life of hardship and pain. But it was ultimately fleeting. Just months later, unfortunately many of her old dramas were back at play.

I had to wonder: Was I in the same state she was in after recovering from her overdose? Open to the world, entranced, amazed, afraid of returning to how I was before—even though I inevitably would? I couldn't believe it, but the memory nagged at me. The program taunted me: *Why do you think you're any different now? You're not. You're really not.*

It all flooded back to me: the fear. The self-medication. The tension I'd been creating in my family. The old stories returned like raindrops on the windshield after the last of them had just been wiped away. I knew this from experience: If I didn't stay clean and stick with the Process, this would all be for nothing.

So that was it then. I had to be better. I had to be better for myself, for my family, and for Mark. Still alive with the beauty of the world around me, I decided I would never go back to how things were. I'd start using the Tools again. I'd start eating better. I'd spend more time with my family. I could do it. I knew I could.

I turned on the couch cushion to face my uncle. "Thank you, Mark. For everything."

He shrugged. "I don't exist."

I smiled because I knew then, finally, that I, too, didn't exist. And that meant I could be anything I wanted to be. I could be the best of me.

* * *

On Saturday, in April, Mark and Nice held the Passover seder, a ritual feast at the beginning of the Jewish holiday of Passover, at their house. Heather, Zachary, and I arrived together.

By this time, the world around me still felt incredibly new. It was like I was walking through the most vivid dream I'd ever experienced. Their dining room table was covered with the traditional seder food items that we would consumc as the story from the Haggadah, the Jewish text that sets forth the order of the seder, progressed, including bitter herbs, vegetables, hard-boiled eggs, charoset (a sweet, dark-colored paste made of fruits and nuts), and roasted chicken wings, as well as wine and matzah. The colors and aromas were stunning, and my mouth felt pulled into a permanent grin.

Once we'd all taken our seats, Mark began leading the seder. He read from a prewritten script, and we'd respond at intervals and sing along to the songs.

Mark interpreted the Exodus story as not just a physical reality but a spiritual one. "If you read the story of Passover and the exodus from Egypt too literally, you're missing the point," Mark said. "It's a metaphor about inner slavery, how I can be a slave to what others think of me or what I think I have to be, having a victim's mindset. But it's an illusion, and I can transcend all of it.

"The story also shows how the slaves, although they were finally freed, complained and wanted to go back to Egypt once things got uncomfortable in the desert. They did not like being in the unknown and would rather suffer and have things be comfortable. The message of Exodus is for us to overcome our ego. Egypt is a code word for our comfort zone, the illusions of who we are and what we're capable of. The pharaoh represents negativity and the desire to receive without sharing with others. The pharaoh is narcissism, selfishness, unkindness.

"The opportunity of Passover," Mark continued, "is to overcome the desire for us to receive for ourselves alone. To transcend the slavery of our minds."

For me, it was to forge a life outside of the trap of the pain amplifier. And for the first time in a long time, I felt ready to do just that.

CHAPTER 10

* * *

The Shift

The unexamined life is not worth living.

—Socrates

In September of the same year, after living in rented apartments and houses for thirteen years, Heather and I purchased our first home together in South Florida, the town where I was born and close to where my parents had raised me. In October, we threw a housewarming party for our closest friends and family to celebrate our first home purchase.

On the morning of the party, I walked through our house—our bedrooms, the bathrooms, the dining room, the kitchen, all with large, high ceilings—feeling the full weight of our blessings press upon me. Heather had made most of the design choices: clean white walls, sand-colored wood floors and tile, blue accents with a coastal vibe. We added deck furniture to our paved courtyard in the back that overlooked a small but beautiful lake.

As I walked around, Zachary was building Lego skyscrapers on the white living room rug, his dirty-blond mop of curly hair falling into his eyes, while Heather made dinner. I wasn't sure what else a man could ask for.

At around 5:30 PM, people began trickling in: my father and stepmother, Heather's parents and sister, Mark and Nice, along with our friends. Soon the house was filled with the din of conversation and the sound of Mark's bellowing laugh. We had an amazing support system around us—just one more thing to be grateful for.

After Heather and I served the food, I sat down at the table and made sure Mark sat to my left. Even when we were just having small talk—about his latest ski trip, about football, about Heather's and my business—my energy noticeably increased. Mark seemed to exude an aura of calm wherever he went.

"Oh, you want to sit with Mark this time?" my dad called from the other side of the table. "Switching things up!"

Nice laughed. "Hey! Alex can give me a break from Mark anytime."

"Amen," Heather said, high-fiving Nice from across the table.

"All right, settle down," Mark said. "I know I'm wonderful, but please, no guilt at the table."

My family often gave me guilt about sticking with Mark

too much at get-togethers, but I couldn't help it. I was already bubbling over with questions I'd wanted to ask him.

"So what do you think about getting old, Mark?"

"It sucks." Mark laughed.

"That doesn't sound so spiritual."

"Reality is what is."

"Well, I don't like it," I said.

"It's all part of the journey."

"I'm just having a hard time seeing the benefits of losing function."

"There are benefits to old age. Now that I'm older, I have some money saved, so I don't have to work as hard. I can enjoy my life. And most of all, wisdom. Have you not benefited from my wisdom and life experiences?"

"I have."

"You see? There is purpose. Aging gives you an opportunity. You can either appreciate each change in your body and life situation or wish them away. And if you can appreciate them, you can help others see the beauty in aging. You can help them find peace with it."

Then I asked Mark about winning and losing. I tended to get upset whenever I lost a tennis match or failed to onboard a new client, and it always knocked me off balance.

"There is no losing because each loss is a learning process," Mark responded.

"But doesn't there have to be a winner and loser?"

"What did I teach you about perception?"

"The world is magic, or something." I smirked at him, taking a sip of my soda.

"Gosh, you are dense, nephew. Perception creates your reality. Winning or losing is a snapshot in time. You're looking at a finite moment and making a final judgment. You're choosing a perception that matches your inner world."

"I'm confused," I said.

"You have a belief about the world being a win or a loss, and you attribute significance to this result. Personally, I don't. I see sport as a fun game. Win, lose—you learn. You grow. Where does your belief about losing coming from?"

I pictured my father in front of the TV, yelling "You bum! You stupid bum!" at his favorite football teams. The memory was funny, but I wondered how much it had informed my perception. I communicated this to Mark. "I guess I think if I lose a game or perform poorly, I must be a loser."

"That's the brightest thing you've said all day. There's hope for you yet." Mark chuckled. "Michael Jordan lost many games, missed big shots. Yet he's called the greatest of all time. In baseball, a great batting average is when you get on base a third of the time. With respect to your dad, that's his world. You can't change that. You don't have to accept that perception."

"Alex, are you complaining about me again?" Dad called. "Can't we just enjoy a nice meal?"

"Love you, Dad!" I shouted back.

He waved a hand at me in mock disgust and got back to eating.

"Something else has been bothering me lately," I said to Mark. "Why do you think bad things happen to good people?"

Mark looked at me seriously. "You don't know the cosmic plan. I've learned you don't always get what you want in life."

He continued, "I had a patient with breast cancer who had to lose her breast. She was very upset and sad. I taught her some of the Process. Reassured her that by changing her perception of the situation, her world would change."

"Did it?"

Mark nodded. "She ended up starting a support group for other women who'd lost a breast, and it completely changed her life. Her life became so full. It gave her a sense of purpose and meaning."

"Receiving in order to share, right?"

"That's right."

We chatted the rest of the dinner, and afterward, my family periodically laughed at us both for being around each other so much. While we were sitting on the couch watching a football game, Mark yelled "You bum!" whenever a Miami Dolphins receiver missed a catch, right alongside my father.

"Wait, I thought there was no such thing as losing?" I said.

"'Do I contradict myself?'" Mark asked. "'Very well, then I contradict myself. I am large, I contain multitudes.' Walt Whitman wrote that. In reality, I don't take it personally. It's a game, a drama, but I don't get pulled into it."

"Come on! You just said my dad acting like that was the cause of my programming about losing."

"It's part of the fun of watching sports, but internally I don't take it seriously. Underneath it all, I understand there are no true wins or losses. But that doesn't stop me from enjoying a good game. Just like it shouldn't stop you from trying to win a tennis match. Some things are just for fun. If we lived completely by higher principles, we might not ever get out of bed!"

I initially resisted this idea, but then I really thought about it. If I wanted to be my most untainted, balanced, and cleanest self, I'd probably have to live in a monastery apart from the rest of the world. Or just waste away meditating at the base of a tree.

I asked, "So it's like how there's a difference between accepting your journey of aging and complaining sometimes about a bad back?"

"Exactly. Just because you believe something at a higher level doesn't mean you won't deal with normal deviations from it in your daily life. Just be careful about where you choose to deviate. When it comes to sports, I have no problems with it."

We turned our attention back to the game. Once it ended and everyone started making their way home, Mark clapped a hand to my shoulder and motioned around the living room. "Congrats on the house, Alex. You really made it. I'm proud of you."

"Yeah, Mark. I did."

I took another look at our home. I glanced at Heather, my beautiful wife, bobbing our son, Zachary, on her knee. I had my JD and my MBA. I had served as a top Tony Robbins coach for about three years. Our business was booming. All of this was true, and I was insanely grateful.

But sometimes I couldn't help feel that something was missing. It wasn't an overpowering feeling, but it was there, and I feared it was getting stronger, ever since the initial euphoria of the Intensive. My throat tightened, and my head started to swim. I walked to the kitchen to make myself another drink. After all, we were celebrating—what was there to be upset about?

* * *

What I call "the shift" happened a couple of months later.

About a week before Christmas, I was on the couch alone watching a show on ABC, already a couple of drinks in. I was about to step outside when something hooked my attention.

The TV showed a 2004 clip from *Good Morning America.* I watched as the co-anchor Dan Harris—a successful, ambitious guy in a dark suit coat, likely wearing stage makeup and hair gel—began to fumble with his words. His voice caught in his throat as he tried to talk about a cholesterol-lowering drug. He looked down at his notes and stopped talking, and then the producers quickly cut back to Diane Sawyer and Charles Gibson.

As I watched the clip, I felt my stomach drop. My heart started to race. I broke out into a sweat. At the same time, my chest was growing tighter while my vision narrowed like a vignette. My breaths were coming in short spurts. It felt like I was having a heart attack. Hyperventilating, I hugged myself and tried to focus on slowing down my breathing, but I couldn't. All I could do was sit there and take it. Finally, after many frightening minutes, the feeling subsided. I wiped the sweat off my face with the front of my T-shirt and took deep breaths into my belly. I felt glued to my spot on the couch, as exhausted as if I'd just played four hours of tennis in the middle of summer.

As I sat on the couch panting, my mind drifted to a trip to Epcot that I'd taken with Heather and Zachary in August, months before. We were riding Spaceship Earth, the slow ride inside the Epcot ball. The ride takes you through the best parts of human history—the first cave painters, the invention of the printing press, the moon landing, the invention of the modern computer. In each scene, old-school animatronic people from each time period painted and wrote and studied and talked, while the English actress Judi Dench narrated a brief history of humankind.

Toward the end of the ride, everything went black, and rows of lights slowly appeared like stars in a black sky. That's when, out of nowhere, my stomach dropped, and I started to feel incredibly afraid. I had no clue what was happening to me, and thankfully it was over in a matter of minutes. When we got off the ride, I got a drink and it settled me down, and

I thought nothing of it afterward. The same thing that was happening to me back then on the ride was now happening again, only worse.

I thought about calling Mark but decided against it. I hadn't been using the Tools, again, and I was beginning to think that he'd been right—I'd used the Intensive to escape, to go through something big without having to put in the work. I'd been so certain that wasn't the case. Was I really that good at fooling myself? And if that were true, it would be too hard to face him.

Then I remembered something he'd told me: *There are no accidents.*

"In the world of the Process, in the world of magic, there is a cause and effect," Mark had said. "For every cause there is an effect, and you must accept responsibility without hesitation. You create your world."

I decided that somehow, I must have created the conditions for this feeling to come into my life. It was clear that I wasn't staying clean or following my training. I kept telling myself I'd quit alcohol and start meditating again, but I didn't follow through. So how couldn't I have contributed to this?

Come on, it was only a couple of episodes over an entire year, I told myself. *Maybe it will just go away on its own. Que sera, sera.*

I switched the TV to Netflix and got up to make another drink.

* * *

For the next week, I didn't sleep. I lay in bed feeling frightened, lonely, dizzy. Sometimes Heather would hold me until the sun came up. Once again, she had become my rock when all I wanted was to be hers.

I started wondering whether the Intensive had triggered all of this. Mark had told me that if I wasn't fully ready to face all the fear at the core of me, it could open me up to things I might not want to deal with. I wondered if this was the effect of that cause. The result of my self-delusion, thinking I wanted to go deeper when really, I wanted to run farther away.

I tried to remind myself that the downs were important because they would allow the new to come. Perhaps it would even be something amazing. The thought helped me get through those nights when my heart wouldn't stop racing and the something inside of me wouldn't stop hissing: *You should've known better. You did this. You've ruined yourself, maybe forever. And your family has to pick up the pieces. What were you thinking?*

On Christmas Eve, I got myself together as best I could to be with family. Heather, Zachary, and I went to my parents' house for their holiday party. Mark and Nice came along too. Again, Mark's energy lifted my mood, but even that couldn't help me totally.

In the middle of dinner, I ran to the bathroom and collapsed on the floor, finding it impossible to breathe. I called for Heather, and she and Mark both came to help. Mark raced to the kitchen and came back with a wheatgrass shot from my parents' stash, which I downed quickly.

"Alex, it's okay. You're having a panic attack," Heather said softly.

"I feel like I'm dying," I gasped.

"You're not going to die." She sounded calm and sure. "This is caused by the effects of adrenaline on sensitized nerves. That's it. Nothing dreadful is going to happen. It never does."

"What do I do?" I was clutching my throat with one hand and had the other on my heaving chest.

"Don't try to control it or stop it. Just stay calm and let it happen. Take deep, slow breaths. Tell yourself, 'Panic if you want. I know what it's like, and it's no big deal.' Breathe into it. It will pass. It always does."

She and Mark stayed with me as the panic subsided. When it was finally over, I told Heather how much her advice helped.

She said, "When we get home, I want you to start reading the book *At Last a Life* by Paul David. It's the only thing that helped me when I was going through this same thing a year or two ago. Paul David doesn't write about panic and anxiety from some theoretical perspective. He dealt with panic, anxiety, and depersonalization for over ten years, trying every medicine he could before he learned to heal himself naturally."

I remembered then that, a few years after Zachary was

born, Heather had experienced anxiety and panic similar to what I was experiencing now. Now, she was there to support me and understand what I was going through.

"Okay, I will," I said. And once I'd calmed down enough, we all returned to celebrate Christmas Eve with the family. Mark even dressed up in a Santa costume as a surprise for the kids.

* * *

That night was just the beginning. The panic attacks continued to come. And come they did—each one seemed more and more vicious. I was so nervous something was wrong with me that I went to the hospital a few times, and they gave me an IV and ran some tests but couldn't find anything out of the ordinary. They prescribed me medications like Xanax and Ativan, but the drugs only seemed to make the panic worse, and I eventually refused to take them.

I repeated to myself that I was not going crazy. And finally, the message sank in: I had to let go. I had to accept the panic and face it. How many times was I going to learn that lesson?

One evening, I lay down in bed and told the panic attacks I wasn't scared anymore. That I would allow them to come. I remembered what Mark had taught me about the pain amplifier, that "fear is the mind killer," and the only way to beat fear is to look it in its eyes. I saw this confrontation as a test, and I was ready for it. To not run from my fear was the microcosm of all experiences, and how I handled the panic attacks would mirror how I'd handle other problems in my life. This was the hologram that Mark had talked about, how the part is then repeated in the whole.

I decided to prove to myself that I would no longer cower in the face of pain and fear. I would face it. I would accept it, no matter what. My number one priority was to master the adrenaline. I knew the signature now: tightness in my upper diaphragm and increased heart rate. All I had to do was breathe slowly and allow the anxiety. It was that simple.

So I did. I accepted all of it. The sweaty palms, racing heart, dizziness, extreme fear. I stayed with my breath through each wave of panic and refused to back down. One after another, the attacks came like water breaking through a dam, and I breathed through each one, using my training to remain balanced and face them with everything I had. Something within me said I wasn't strong enough. Part of me doubted why I was even putting myself through this. But I stayed with the waves, the breath, the presence, as much as I could.

Nothing dreadful is going to happen, I thought as fear spread its cold fingers through my body. *This is just adrenaline. I'm not going anywhere. Panic if you want to. I know what it's like. It's no big deal. I will let it pass through me.*

In total, I experienced four panic attacks that night. By not fighting the adrenaline and accepting it and letting it exhaust itself, Heather was right—I could stop the cycle.

I'd let fear have too much ground, just like I had when

I was in college dealing with my unhealthy attachment to Rachel. Now, once again, it was time to take my life back, little by little.

* * *

As I had suspected, that night was only the first battle.

When Mark called to check on me about a week after I panicked at the Christmas party, I didn't know what to say. I didn't want to disappoint him, but not even the Process had seemed to be able to take me out of this all-consuming yet nonsensical terror in my body. Though the panic was gone, the anxiety was only worsening week by week.

One night, Zachary asked me to play Legos with him, so we plopped onto the rug together, and I grabbed the bucket of Legos from beside the TV stand and poured them onto the carpet. As he stacked Lego bricks, one after the other, I could barely sit still. I scratched my arms, bounced my legs, and clicked Legos together. But it didn't help. I couldn't do it. I couldn't just be there with him. I had to get up and go for a walk.

That's when I knew I had to get this under control. I didn't want to be that kind of father. I wanted to be there for my son. It was like I'd pulled a muscle in my mind, and I felt the sting of it constantly. But if that were true, it should heal over time when I just gave it a break. If I supported its healing. Even though I'd turned the corner when I confronted the attacks, my mind was apparently still injured.

Of course, this condition was only a microcosm of something much bigger. My habits had to change. Not only would I overcome the anxiety, but I'd make my entire life better. Less stressful, more present, more loving.

The truth is that it took me time to come to terms with anxiety. Almost two years, in fact.

I began to wonder whether these emotions wanted me to let go, but my fixation on how bad I felt caused them to stubbornly hang on. Once again, I had to wonder if I had brought this reality upon myself. The thought was as unwelcome as always, but I had to believe it was true. Because how many times had I already seen that truth for myself?

It was a sluggish, often agonizing process to claw my way out of that hole. But with every swipe, I slowly improved my mind and perception once again. The breakthrough was about to begin.

CHAPTER 11

* * *

Rebirth

The purpose of our lives is to be happy.

—Dalai Lama

A few weeks later, I walked into my garage for a morning meditation. Though my garage was much neater than Mark's and filled with tennis equipment, the two atmospheres had lately begun to feel similar. I felt calm here, centered, like good intentions were in the air.

I left the light off in the windowless garage so that only a sliver of illumination peeked through the door to the house. I sat in a red camping chair and steadied my breathing, paying attention to birdsong and every frog croaking outside the garage door.

I closed my eyes and began to meditate when I felt something building in me, in my chest. Something that felt chaotic. I peered in, and suddenly I was visualizing myself falling again through that tunnel of earth, the same one I'd found myself in two years ago during the Intensive. The same roots, rocks, and plants in the earthen walls flew past me as I fell farther downward. The same hateful voice hissed beside me, *You're a mess. Two years of all this pain—for what? You're nothing, Alex. Why are you even here? What are you even for?*

Unlike last time, I didn't scream. I didn't claw at the wall trying to find my footing. I didn't recite prayers or call for my wife. Instead, I got curious. I turned my head to see where the voice was coming from. I wanted to know what hated me so much and why. I knew it was some part of me, but I also knew it was only one part.

What I saw, falling with me, was a monstrous dragon. This must have been the entity I'd seen before in my dreams. I could tell from its sharp yellow eyebrows and smoking nostrils that it hated me. It *really* hated me.

It continued to taunt me. *You're nothing. You're not there for your family. You pretend to be spiritual. You're a coward.*

I wanted to hide my face in my hands. I wanted to open my eyes and stop the meditation. I wanted to never look at this beast again. But I didn't move an inch. I decided to let it say whatever it wanted to. I could look at it squarely now, and now I had something to say.

I kept my body relaxed and open, palms facing forward, no tensing or protecting, even as we both continued to fall. "I'm not afraid of you," I said. "I'm not running anymore."

Unfazed, it roared at me, spit flying in my face, a small fire forming at the back of its throat. It was almost ready to kill me.

But I just smiled at it. I even laughed, despite myself. "You think you're my master, but you're not. I'm yours."

With that, the fire instantly died in its mouth. Its sharp face morphed from hatred to confusion and finally to what looked like a hint of desperate sadness. Its body went limp.

We fell to the ground at the same time, though neither of us was harmed. The dragon immediately scurried into a corner of what I again recognized to be my childhood living room. It curled up on itself, looking more like a frightened garden lizard than a fierce beast. I sat down beside the dragon and began to stroke its skin. The scales along its back were surprisingly soft.

"What do you want?" I asked. "Why are you here?"

The dragon's voice was muted, almost a whisper. It barely moved its lips when it said, "I don't know. I think I *used* to know."

"If you used to know, you can know again."

The dragon thought about that for a minute and then nodded.

"How can I help you figure it out?" I asked.

Its big red eyes rolled toward me. "Can you tell me a story? A good one. A happy one."

So I did. I told the story of a young boy and the magician who changed his life.

After I'd finished the story, ending with the complications of Heather and me having our baby, the dragon asked, "And how is the boy now?"

"Even better," I said. "A lot better."

The dragon sighed, smoke still curling from its nose, and then told me what it wanted. "It's obvious. I just wanted to protect you, Alex. But you wouldn't look at me. You wouldn't hear me. I had to make you listen however I could."

I told the dragon I understood, and I did. It was an animal in a locked room. Things go crazy in the dark. How couldn't they?

Before my eyes, the dragon began to shrink, its scales turning to fur and its claws becoming paws. Now, it was an injured wolf, one leg bleeding from a nasty gash. It was howling like mad. I tore off a strip of my T-shirt and wrapped the injury, then let the wolf climb onto my lap. It whined softly as I held it.

As I sat with the wolf, petting it, I put a hand on my heart and felt my own life energy. I heard something in the far recesses of my mind say, *I can allow all of this to be this way as long as it needs to be.* And with that, I could feel a wave of energy resonate throughout my body, starting from the sitting base traveling up my torso, through my arms, and up to the top of my head. I felt expansive, loving, open. I continued to caress the wolf while keeping my hand on my chest. I breathed deeply for a few more moments.

Then, even the wolf began to shrink. And when it was over, I was holding Mordi, my old dog, in my arms. Mordi was dying again, and I let him, even as I wept. I told him I couldn't wait to see him again. I told him that I would never forget him.

Just as his body went limp, Mordi inexplicably burst into life once again, as healthy as I'd ever seen him. He wanted to play, jumping from my lap and barking, his tail a propeller-like blur. I found a rope in the corner of the room and played tug-of-war with him, feeling happy, full, certain. I stayed in this space, playing with Mordi for a long time.

Slowly, the vision faded away. The chirping and buzzing outside the garage doors came back into my awareness. I noticed a powerful warmth flowing through my entire body, like the blood was rushing back into me from somewhere else. When I felt ready, I opened my eyes. The garage lights flickered.

Everything looked beautiful, just as it had after the Intensive. I didn't feel free of the past. Instead, I felt incredibly *here. Present.* Incredibly *okay* with everything that had ever happened to me and ever would happen. I realized that anxiety isn't about what you are feeling but what you are *refusing* to feel. The dread that had plagued me for so long had dissipated, but I didn't fear it returning. In fact, I knew it would come back, and I even welcomed it. Perhaps I would see it as an opportunity to go deeper once again, to find another subjugated part of myself and invite it into the fray.

The feeling reminded me of finally letting Rachel go all those years ago. How great it had felt to release an old story, an old drama. This had been the next level in what I was beginning to learn was the constant push in the growth of the Process. I began to wonder if I ever *wasn't* following the Process. Even when I felt powerless to change my perception, Mark's teachings never left me. Instead, they reminded me of the person I could be with enough discipline, desire, and belief in the kind of magic he knew so well.

Two of Mark's stories came to me at that moment.

One: We once watched the movie *A Beautiful Mind* together. It's the story of John Nash, a mathematical genius who developed schizophrenia later in his life and struggled with hallucinations of people. Mark pointed out that the movie didn't end with the main character banishing the voices in his head—it ended with him learning to live with those voices. That was the exact lesson it had taken me so long to learn, which I'd perhaps be learning for the rest of my life.

Two: Mark had had to endure the same trials as I did. He'd had to see his Inner Self and realize how he'd been treating it, and he had to do it alone. In the end, I had to face the programs alone, just like he'd said I would at the beginning of my journey with the Process.

And I'd done it. I'd looked at my own self-hatred, my own fear, my own sadness, pain, and discomfort, and watched them transform through love and attention into my friend. I realized that sometimes opposing the dark side doesn't look like a knight with a sword in his hand, but like a kid offering a flower to a stranger on the street—or me helping my inner dragon recover from deep wounds. Compassion is its own kind of opposition to darkness.

I wanted to welcome every exiled part of me, every animal within me that I'd allowed to be filled with darkness. But I felt no hurry to do it. I knew that the darkness had no choice but to reveal itself with time, and I'd face each beast as it raised its head. So instead, I went back inside to be with my family.

Right when I walked into the house, Heather called me from the office upstairs.

"What's up?" I asked as I stood behind her computer chair, rubbing her shoulders.

"Something unbelievable," she said. "Look at this post I just saw."

She showed me a listing on a pet adoption site. My jaw literally dropped, and the warmth in my chest intensified. "This can't be real. Is this real?"

Heather looked back at me. "If this doesn't make you believe in coincidences."

She had been looking at dogs for a while. A few months after Mordi's death, we bought a golden retriever named Murphy to fill the void of not having a dog in our home. We figured we needed a big, sturdy, kind dog since we had a very active toddler on our hands. But Murphy needed a lot of attention, and we could not give it to her the way she needed it. Heather and I thought it might be a good idea to get another dog, so Murphy could have a friend and companion.

That day, Heather decided to look up adoptable dogs. Well, apparently, the first listing she pulled up was not just any dog—it was a Jack Russell terrier. This dog happened to be available right away for adoption and was no more than two miles away from our home at a foster care house. The really incredible thing was that he had almost the exact same markings and prayer cap spot on his head as our old dog, Mordi. And even stranger than that was: This dog was named Morty. Same name, just a different spelling.

Heather called the person in charge of the foster company and spoke with the woman immediately. She told us that Morty had been wandering the streets and gotten hit by a car, only to be found by a woman and her son who couldn't keep him because of apartment restrictions.

Heather looked up from her phone and said we could go meet the dog at the place where they were fostering him. Heather then said, "The former owner of the dog made one request: that Morty go to a house with a young child since her son is going to miss him."

I shook my head incredulously. "A Jack Russell named Morty who needs a house with a kid . . . What are the chances?"

Heather turned the chair around to face me and said, "We can visit him tomorrow. So? What do you think?"

I knelt down in front of Heather, then glanced again at the dog's kind amber eyes, the blur of his tail that had clearly been wagging. Mark had called something like this *synchronicity*—

a kind of coincidence but one with meaning, with a message. I had trouble figuring out what the hell else it could be.

"Mordi 2.0," I said. "You know, I think Zachary will love him."

Heather wrapped her arms around me and leaned in for a kiss. "Me too."

The next day, we visited the foster home, and we all fell in love with Morty immediately. We brought him home that afternoon. Within a few moments, he started chasing our son around the house, making Zachary laugh like crazy, and we knew it was the right thing.

* * *

A few weeks later, I arrived at Fort Lauderdale Beach just as the sun was rising above the sea. The light was murky since the clouds were thick, threatening rain, as I walked down the boardwalk. I noticed Mark's silhouette straight ahead of me, looking grayish in the morning light. When I reached the sand, I pulled off my sandals and carried them. I watched a jogger pass behind Mark and slow down slightly, turning her head curiously in his direction.

I sat down beside Mark on the big red towel he'd laid out only about ten feet from the incoming tide. Mark sat cross-legged, his feet resting on opposite legs. A sun hat shaded his eyes. Sitting next to him, I felt an aura of calm instantly overtake me.

"So, Mark," I said, "what's on the agenda for today? Hot-coal walking? Ritual sacrifice?"

"Fresh out of coals." He laughed lightly. "But I do have some things to share with you. Alex, did I ever tell you my purpose as a doctor when I see my patients?"

"I don't know. Do no harm?"

"You're a comedian today! No, it's energy. When a patient leaves my office, my goal is that they leave with more energy than they came in with. That energy can be hope, it can be compassion, it can be something I taught them. It's not just my 'job' to be a physician. Being a physician is the role I play. But being a conduit of energy, making the world around me better—that is the core of what we all can do."

"I feel it when I'm around you. You seem to affect the environment you're in just by existing there."

"You're beginning to do the same, Alex. I can tell something's really different in you. You're becoming your own master now."

"I hope so. But it's hard to believe in it. In all this, sometimes. How do I know the Process is true? That it isn't just coincidences and dumb good luck?"

"It's your choice," Mark replied. "Remember our first lesson."

I recited the main premise of the Process for the hundredth time: "The world is an illusion, it works by magic, and the magic is perception."

"Yes. You can choose to live in a world where there is magic, where things happen by your intention. Or you can live in a world of chaos and randomness. It's up to you: You can live in a supportive universe where things happen for a positive reason or one where it doesn't."

"I want to live in a world with magic."

He smiled, his eyes crinkling up. "So do I. Consider this. Nice and I were visiting Brazil, her home country, when she couldn't find her wedding ring. We looked all over—in the luggage, all around the house, everywhere, but we couldn't find it.

"Well, we'd heard about a technique from Kabbalah, an esoteric school of thought in Jewish mysticism and also an aspect of the Process, called the *72 Names of God*. Each of the 72 names has a certain frequency. It was helpful to meditate on them in order to achieve some objective.

"We decided to do exactly that on our big meditation day, Saturday. We focused and meditated on those *72 Names of God* to find the ring. After an hour, Nice got out of meditation and walked into the bathroom. She opened up the doors underneath the sink, and when she did, a small bag fell out and into her hand. It contained her ring."

"Magic," I said.

"That's what I think too."

Mark looked toward the water, the waves rushing forth and retreating in front of us. I sensed that he wasn't done talking, so I stayed quiet and buried my feet in the sand in front of me.

"Someday I won't be here," he said solemnly. "You'll have to find the answers within. But you need a reliable way to do it. You can't go down the rabbit hole every time you need an answer. So I have one more thing to teach you."

"I can't imagine my life without you," I said. "I don't even want to think about it."

"That time will come. But when you need an answer and I'm not here, you can use the Huna Prayer."

"What's that?"

"Huna is Hawaiian for 'hidden' or 'secret.' It's another Tool we use in the Process when uncertain about what to do next. I'll walk you through it this time. First, begin to meditate."

I closed my eyes and began to breathe deeply. The whooshing of the waves intensified in my ears, as did the seagulls cackling and the pattering of a jogger's footsteps every so often. The smell of salty air with a tinge of seaweed and fish filled my nostrils.

"Once you're balanced, think of a question," Mark said. "Something you really want the answer to."

Instantly I knew what it would be: *How can I best share the gift that Mark has given me?* I held it in my mind as I waited for Mark's next instruction.

"Now, recalling what I taught you about the law of three selves, visualize your Middle Self going to the altar of your Higher Self. Have your Middle Self ask this question."

In my mind, the altar was a grand piano with its casing closed and several lit votive candles atop it. The piano was surrounded by scattered hibiscus flowers and sprigs of rosemary. I knelt down at this piano altar and focused on my question: *How can I best share the gift that Mark has given me?*

"Once you've done that, have your Inner Self go to the altar and give a sacrifice. The sacrifice must be some kind of forgiveness, you forgiving anyone or anything. It has to be real. It can be as big as someone who hurt one of your loved ones, or as small as someone who cut you off in traffic. But it has to be real."

I saw a young version of me appear to my left, wearing overalls and a blue-and-red-striped shirt. He cupped his hand over my ear and whispered a name. *Of course*, I thought. *Who else needed more of my forgiveness? Who else had I blamed for so much, again and again?*

The week before, I'd taken Zachary over to my mother's house. She was no longer the bubbly, wide-eyed person she'd been when we found ourselves at the zoo in front of the orangutan exhibit a few years ago. The experience of the overdose *had* changed her. And to this day, she hasn't touched drugs since. She now lives contentedly with her two cats near us in South Florida.

As we both watched Zachary play, I'd said, "You seem good, Mom."

"Today I am." Her smile had been small but genuine. Her curly brown hair was now shorter, extending out in all directions, and she wore a floral purple tank top. "We'll see what tomorrow brings."

I'd thought to grab her hand or put a hand on her shoulder, but it didn't feel right. "I'm sorry about how I treated you when you came down after the overdose. I want you to know that I don't want to change you. I just want you to be happy."

She was silent for a moment before responding, her eyes on Zachary. "You know, maybe I am. Not Hollywood happy, maybe. No big feelings. But I think I'm my own kind of happy."

"How's that?"

"Well, I guess because I have everything I need. This house, my cats, my family . . . My life's not perfect, but it's not chaos anymore either. It's just . . . content. And I like it this way."

"That's so great, Mom."

"Seeing you happy makes me happy too." She'd put a hand on my shoulder then and smiled at me briefly before turning back to Zachary.

"And vice versa," I'd said.

"It comes and goes in waves, Alex. Maybe it always will. Can't that be okay?"

Que sera, sera, I'd said to myself. *Never too high nor too low.* Considering everything Mark had taught me, I knew it was okay.

"I think so," I said. "I love you, Mom."

"I love you too."

So, on that beach with Mark, I knew I was already close to finding the space in my heart to truly accept my mother, in a way I wasn't able to in my youth. In my mind, I spoke the words aloud to the altar: *Mom, I forgive you. For everything. You were in so much pain. You did your very best. I want to let my pain go now. I choose to be at peace with you now.*

I'd said these words so many times before, yet this time, I felt an incredible lightness with them. Like I *really* meant them.

Mark's voice was low and calm beside me. "As you continue to meditate, the answer to your question will come to you."

As I watched the altar, the piano keys began to depress lightly on their own. The tune was "Earth Angel," a 1950s song that was one of Mark's favorites. As the piano played as if by magic, something was beginning to become clear.

A big part of me doubted myself. Who was I to share this story, the one of my uncle the magician and all that I'd learned from him, or to pretend that I could teach other people? I'm not enlightened. I'm not perfect. I haven't figured it all out. And I may continue to go through periods of abandoning the Tools and the Process altogether.

But then my Higher Self spoke: I should come before others not claiming to know it all, but rather knowing that I've been blessed by the Process. That a great man, a guide, and a teacher has bestowed upon me a gift. I'm not the guru—I am simply a messenger. Mark taught me to receive in order to share, to make the world around me better and thus make my world better. My purpose isn't to know it all—it's to share what I know generously and to the best of my abilities.

I recalled the story of the prodigal son. In the parable, a son is given an inheritance and goes off to squander the money. He comes back to his father destitute. When his father accepts him back, the young man is changed.

I was given an inheritance, the Process. I squandered it. I stopped using the Tools. Subsequently, I was alone in the dark for a while, but I returned. And the Process welcomed me back. Now, as a result, the knowledge and training were clearer and more integrated.

All the experiences along the way had been opportunities, as my uncle would've told me. I got what I needed, not what I wanted. Not having a strong mother figure gave me my uncle Mark, the magician. The difficult breakup with my first girlfriend gave me the Process, and then Heather and Zachary. The dark night period gave me a deep connection to my inner world, great love and compassion for the darkest parts of me, and a newfound appreciation for life. There were no accidents.

I opened my eyes and shared what I'd learned with my uncle.

"Wonderful, my nephew," Mark said. "Now you're living a real life. You see that my job was not to give you love but to give you independence. Now you can heal yourself. You can lead yourself. And you can share your gifts with others."

"Thank you," I said. "I'm so appreciative of what you've done for me."

"My pleasure."

"Wait, you aren't going to say you don't exist?"

"Do I exist?"

We both laughed good and long.

Then Mark clapped a hand on my shoulder and stood up. "I'm headed out to work. But first, Alex, I'm curious. Many years ago you said you were working on a book project about your experience of the Process. How's that coming along?"

A wave of warmth rushed through me. "You're right. Maybe it's time to make it happen."

"Oh, one more thing," Mark said.

My uncle reached his hands up toward the heavy storm clouds and, looking up, squinted his eyes tight. Impossibly, the clouds began to race toward the east, until they had dissipated completely, and the sun was bright on our skin.

I turned toward Mark, stunned. "Did you do that?"

He glanced back at me, his eyes now full of light. "This world is ruled by magic, Alex," he said. "Who knows what we are truly capable of?"

The Process Summaries

The Premises

- The world is an illusion, it works by magic, and the magic is perception. As you change your perception, you change your world. This is true magic.
- By making the world around you better, you make your life better.
- The greatest thing you can give anyone is independence.

The Tools

Always remember: Materials first.

1. Wheatgrass
2. Walking
3. Meditation

Get free access to additional resources:
https://alexnottingham.com/tools/.

Teachings and Lessons

BE CLEAN: Treat people with respect, treat your body with respect, and avoid manipulating others. Be vigilant, generous, kind, and aware. One slipup, and it's Humpty Dumpty—you can't fix it.

BREAD OF SHAME: Avoid bread of shame by earning what you get.

BULLY: Never back down to a bully. You must stand up for what is right as it builds character.

CARDS YOU ARE DEALT: Life gives you certain circumstances. Maximize how you make the best of what you're given.

CAUSE AND EFFECT: For every cause, there is an effect, and you must accept responsibility without hesitation.

CERTAINTY: Trust in the power of certainty. When you act in good faith and put in the work, things will always work out how they're supposed to.

CHOICE: You can choose to live in a world where there is magic, where things happen by your intention, or you can live in a world of chaos and randomness. You can live in a supportive universe where things happen for a positive reason or one where it doesn't.

CROSS-SEX SELF: When you're unkind to someone of the

opposite sex, you're being unkind to that energy within you. Don't harm your cross-sex self.

DARKNESS: Darkness follows the light. Wherever there is goodness, the evil will attempt to sabotage it. Be prepared.

DOG IN A LOCKED ROOM: Suppressing your feelings just makes them stronger.

DOUBT: Doubt is the dark's greatest weapon. Exercise your trust and certainty.

THE FARMER: Never get too high or too low.

FEAR: Fear is an illusion. You must take control of it and use it for growth, not let it destroy you.

HELP: One should not help someone who doesn't want to be helped. By doing so, one strips the other of their free will.

HOLOGRAM: The world is a hologram. The small reflects the whole.

LOSING: There is no losing because each loss is a learning process.

MIRROR: Everyone around you is a mirror. Only you exist in your world.

NEED: You don't always get what you want, but you do get what you need.

OTHERS' THINGS: Treat others' things with even more respect than you treat your own.

QUE SERA, SERA: Do the best you can and allow the universe to unfold as it will.

SIMPLIFYING: Making the complex simple allows you to teach others.

STOP: When you're unbalanced, say the four-letter word: "STOP." Think about what you're doing and what you should be doing. This moves you from a reactive Inner Self to a proactive Middle Self.

TANGENT: It's important that you define what it is you're talking about.

THREE SELVES: Your psyche is divided into three selves: Your Inner Self is memory and emotion, your Middle Self is your reason, and your Higher Self is a connection to source, the universe, and God (whatever that means to you).

The "Five Steps for Creating a World"

1. **Desire: The starting point of every creation.** Reconnect to your will. (Higher Self)
2. **Mechanism: Gather the training, tools, and structure.** Once the aim is clear, identify the concrete mechanisms—skills, systems, mentors, and resources—that will carry your idea from concept to reality. The right mechanism turns passion into an executable plan. (Middle Self)
3. **Enthusiasm: It has to be fun or enjoyable.** Focus on what excites you, so the work stays fresh and sustainable. (Inner Self)
4. **Work: Put in the disciplined, consistent effort.**

There are no shortcuts. Show up, log the hours, and "go the extra mile." (Middle Self)

5. **Receive: Gratefully accept and integrate the rewards.** Paradoxically, many people miss this step. Celebrate your results. You earned it. You are worthy. Resist the self-sabotage program. Gratitude completes the cycle and prepares you for the next creation. (All Selves)

The Huna Prayer

Go into meditation. Visualize your Middle Self going to the altar of the Higher Self and asking a question about whatever you need to know. Then have your Inner Self go to the altar of the Higher Self and give a sacrifice. The sacrifice must be in the form of a forgiveness—for example, forgiving the dog for an accident on the rug or the guy who cut in front of you in traffic. Then be patient in meditation, and the answers will come to you.

Teaching Movies for the Process

- *Dune*
- *Krull*

Acknowledgments

First and foremost, I wish to thank my incredible wife—my life partner—who has been my constant source of love, encouragement, and inspiration. Her steadfast support in all aspects of my life, including this very book, has been immeasurable, and I am profoundly grateful for the ways she lifts me up every day.

I also extend my heartfelt gratitude to my family and friends, whose unwavering belief in me has fueled my determination in all my endeavors. Their presence and reassurance have guided me through challenges, reminding me that I am never alone on this journey.

A special thank you to my father, who sparked my early love for knowledge and instilled in me a sense of curiosity that has carried me through life. His dedication to learning and exploration helped shape my educational path. He was there when I needed him most, always showing up, always believing in me—even when I didn't believe in myself.

To my mother, thank you for the love and time you gave me, especially when life didn't make it easy. You overcame so much. You are an inspiration to me to never give up on oneself and to appreciate life.

To my stepmother, thank you for your quiet and unwavering support throughout the years—often without recognition or reward. It fills me with joy and deep appreciation that my two mothers share not only mutual respect but a genuine friendship. That, in itself, is a kind of magic.

To my son, Zachary, thank you for being a teacher to me. Being able to see life through your eyes with your own inherent wisdom and humor is a blessing. May you be happy and have peace of mind. May you be a light to others.

And finally, my deepest thanks go to my uncle Mark, the magician, who taught me that wonder and possibility lie at the heart of every new discovery. He inspired me to think beyond the ordinary, inviting a bit of magic into everyday life.

To each of you, I owe more than these words can convey. Thank you for joining me on this adventure.

About the Author

Alex Nottingham, JD, MBA, is an entrepreneur, speaker, attorney, and bestselling author. A former top Tony Robbins coach, he now guides professionals toward greater purpose and fulfillment through evidence-based business and personal-growth strategies.

He is certified in mindfulness-based stress reduction (MBSR) and neuro-linguistic programming (NLP). He actively practices relationship-based focusing, internal family systems (IFS), and insight meditation.

Alex is the visionary and CEO of All-Star Dental Academy and host of the *Dental All-Stars* podcast, together reaching more than 100,000 professionals annually. He holds both a JD and an MBA from Florida International University.

He lives in Florida with his wife, Heather, their son, Zachary, and two dogs: Murphy, a golden retriever, and Morty, a Jack Russell terrier.

His website is https://alexnottingham.com.